Robert Ainslie Redford

Four Centuries of Silence

Or from Malachi to Christ

Robert Ainslie Redford

Four Centuries of Silence
Or from Malachi to Christ

ISBN/EAN: 9783337165369

Printed in Europe, USA, Canada, Australia, Japan

Cover: Foto ©Lupo / pixelio.de

More available books at **www.hansebooks.com**

FOUR CENTURIES OF SILENCE;

OR,

FROM MALACHI TO CHRIST.

FOUR CENTURIES OF SILENCE;

OR,

FROM MALACHI TO CHRIST.

BY THE

REV. R. A. REDFORD, M.A., LL.B.,

PROFESSOR OF SYSTEMATIC THEOLOGY AND APOLOGETICS, NEW COLLEGE, LONDON ;

AUTHOR OF "THE CHRISTIAN'S PLEA AGAINST MODERN UNBELIEF,"
"STUDIES IN THE BOOK OF JONAH," ETC. ETC.

CHICAGO:

JANSEN McCLURG & CO.,

117 WABASH AVENUE.

1885.

PREFACE.

THE aim of this volume, it will be understood from the title, is to characterise a period, rather than to set forth a history. The author has no claim to be regarded as having thrown any new light, by independent researches, on questions, some of which are involved in much obscurity. But he has brought together, within a limited space, a number of facts, which will serve to confirm the faith of those who accept the authority of Scripture, while they illustrate the wonderful method of Divine Providence, in preparing the way for the higher revelations of Christianity.

Too little attention has been given by the students of revelation to the deeply interesting subjects briefly sketched in these pages. The author has been led by this consideration to write these chapters, which appeared as separate papers in a monthly periodical.[1] He publishes

1 *The Homiletic Magazine.*

them now, in a collected form, in the hope that they will open the way, in some minds, to a deeper study of the state of the Jewish Church during the long period intervening between the Old and New Testaments. He is not without the conviction that such a study will do much to promote the cause of Truth. The whole question of revelation is one of profound and momentous interest in the present day. It is one which will never be firmly and finally settled on any other than an historical basis.

Putney, *July* 13, 1885.

CONTENTS.

CHAP.   PAGE

I. THE LAST OF THE PROPHETS 1

II. THE JEWISH PONTIFICATE 16

III. THE COURT OF THE GENTILES 36

IV. THE SEPTUAGINT 59

V. THE APOCRYPHA 81

VI. THE SCRIBES AND THEIR TRADITIONS 102

VII. THE RISE OF JEWISH SECTS 125

VIII. THE GROWTH OF THE MESSIANIC EXPECTATION . . 145

IX. THE JEWISH SANHEDRIM 169

X. PHILO OF ALEXANDRIA 192

XI. THE DAWNING LIGHT 216

XII. THE VOICE IN THE WILDERNESS 238

FOUR CENTURIES OF SILENCE;

OR,

FROM MALACHI TO CHRIST.

CHAPTER I.

THE LAST OF THE PROPHETS.

THE two volumes which now stand side by side in our Bible, preserve, in their separate titles, the memory of a great gulf of time, dividing the *old* from the *new*. Four hundred years is a long period in the history of any nation. They were eventful years in the annals of the Jewish people. Is it possible, we naturally ask, that during all that time no gleams of Truth should have come forth upon the sky ? There was once, in the age of the great prophets, a bright glow of spiritual glory spreading along the horizon ; faith and hope and love flaming in the souls of lofty-minded men, full of patriotic ardour, and ecstatic visions of the future, breathing the highest strains of poetic rap-

A

ture, and lifting up the people of God into a prayerful expectation of the coming day.

That wonderful evening sky continued to cheer true hearts through centuries of trouble and change. The captives of Israel and Judah, scattered over Eastern lands, divided from one another, mourning over the desolation of their homes, and bitterly repenting the ages of unfaithfulness which had culminated in so gloomy a destiny of judgment, still, through the long sad years of exile, kept before them the lovely tints of prophetic radiance; they spoke to them of a rising Sun of Righteousness, which should bring with it the day of salvation. The seventy years of Judah's banishment went by. The time of restoration arrived. Band after band of exiles returned to Palestine. For a hundred years the history of the Jewish people was the history of a reawakening nationality. But the sky was not again lighted up with the same brilliancy. The colours seemed to fade. There were prophets still sent to accompany the work of restoration. *Zerubbabel* had his *Zechariah* and his *Haggai.* But the glow of the prophetic inspiration was rather declining than increasing. At last the New Jerusalem seemed to be complete. The energetic measures of the Persian cup-bearer, Nehemiah, filled with zeal for his beloved land, had raised up the fallen city, and re-established the neglected Temple service. The land had rest; and the people could look away from the sphere of their earthly environment to the heaven of their hopes. Once more, as the faithful reformer (Nehemiah) set his diligent hand to the building up of their civil and religious establishment, there was a new light shooting across the sky, and brightening the horizon with fresh colours of Divine appeal and invitation. It was not so rich and glowing as that which flamed like a fire three hundred years before, but which had since so much faded from the view of the people. But it was still beyond all doubt a heavenly gift. And after that evening of prophecy there followed a night of four hundred years; during which it was only here and there that the sky was faintly illuminated by some star of wise, devout reflection, borrowing its light from the past, but pointing on very distinctly to the future.

We learn much from the study of that remarkable silence of prophecy in Israel. We are able to distinguish all the more clearly the voice of God when it did certainly speak. We call on the Jews themselves to be our witnesses, that in putting the New Testament beside the Old we are not dishonouring the fathers, but giving them their

true place, while we are hailing the risen glory
of the day of grace.   There were many writers
after the time of the Old Testament.   But there
was no *prophet* after him whose words were
placed by the Jews themselves at the end of their
Scriptures.   Why did they thus distinguish between their *prophets* and their *scribes ?*   Was it
not because there arose no messenger whose words
and ministry seemed to them at all like those who
had gone before ?   The sacred volume of the Old
Testament was put together by the labours of
Ezra, Nehemiah, and others of their contemporaries.
And the reverence which immediately gathered
about the collection of sacred writings became a
"hedge" about it, not to be broken through.   From
that time nothing but the surpassing claims of an
inspired teacher, who manifestly came from God,
would lift up any of his words into the sky.   And
alas! the formalism of the schools, the cloudy
disputations of the Rabbis, the mists of earthly
disorders and national decay floating upwards,
obscured more and more the light of the horizon,
until the time of the *sunrising* came, when there
was again the *morning glow* that " prepared the
way of the Lord."

Let us, then, first take our stand at that point
of time which is indicated by the close of the Old

Testament canon ; and let us look at that *evening sky of the Jewish Church,* lighted up as it was by the last gleam of prophetic inspiration in the words of the Prophet Malachi.

Although the fiery trial of the Babylonish captivity completely removed from the Jewish nation all the dross of idolatry in the form of pagan rites and worship of pagan deities, it by no means delivered them from the temptation to which they were still exposed, to put their trust in that which was a *means of grace,* but not necessarily *grace itself.* The Levitical Restoration brought back the law of Moses into its place of supremacy. The rebuilding of the Temple, and recommencement of Temple services and national festivals, renewed in the minds of the people the sense of their peculiar vocation as a consecrated and holy nation, to offer sacrifices continually unto Jehovah, acceptable in His sight because of His gracious election. But while the first glory of the reformation glowed, no doubt, very brightly through all the land, and hopes were kindled afresh in all hearts that the time of their triumph was approaching, generation followed generation, and the climax was still delayed. We can easily imagine that the first zeal of the newly-founded nation began to grow cold ; the legal prescriptions faded out of recollection, and the Temple lost somewhat of its attraction. The children of those who surrounded Zerubbabel were less enthusiastic than their fathers. The grandchildren began to grow weary in their religious services. And when Nehemiah, in the century following that of the return of the captives, rebuilt the ruins of Jerusalem, he found it necessary to take stern and even fierce measures to enforce the observance of the law, and to purify the Temple from defilers. During his absence in Persia the people had fallen back into disorder. "And I came to Jerusalem, and understood of the evil that Eliashib did for Tobiah in preparing him a chamber in the courts of the house of God. And it grieved me sore: therefore I cast forth all the household stuff of Tobiah out of the chamber. Then I commanded, and they cleansed the chambers: and thither brought I again the vessels of the house of God, with the meat offering and the frankincense. Then contended I with the rulers, and said, Why is the house of God forsaken?" (Neh. xiii. 7-9, 11). As a result from this laxness in religious observance, the social bonds of the people were being loosened. For it must be remembered that for the Jews to become careless of their Temple and of their law was not to rise *above* that legal economy, but to fall *below* it. Just as there is many a man still, who forsakes the accustomed place of worship, not because he is living a more spiritual life and is able to dispense with an external form, but because the sense of the Divine, the need of an outlet of worshipping feelings, is gone. So, a hundred years after the restoration of the Mosaic system under Zerubbabel, Ezra and Nehemiah found that the *moral* life of the Jews was sinking rapidly, in the decay of *religious* institutions. There was one survival of the captivity, however, which, though it was scarcely likely that the zealous reformers should appreciate all its importance, contributed much to preserve the spiritual element of the people. That was the practice of meeting together in *synagogue*. It had grown up into a general and well-established religious institution, during the time of exile; though it doubtless took a fresh start in the new circumstances of the restoration, especially during the time of Ezra, when the study of the ancient Scriptures, and their diffusion among the people, induced many to seek the public assembly and the exposition of God's Word by wise and learned men. Thus "the Word of God and prayer" came to be regarded as the substance of religion. There are indications, as early as the time of Elisha the prophet, that the people gathered together, *on occasion*, to listen to exhortations elsewhere than in the Temple. The long suspension of the Temple services during the Captivity would call out such occasional services into more regular observance. And the large number of psalms attributed to the same period of the exile, points to the congregational worship as that which then prevailed. Thus, at the close of the fifth century before Christ, the two facts meet us in the history : on the one hand, the general *decline of religious observance and moral health* among the people ; and on the other, the appearance of a *congregational worship* which, while it promoted the growth of the Rabbinical spirit, and the class of scribes and learned doctors, did yet, at the same time, nourish the development of individual piety, and knowledge of the *Word of God*.

These remarks will prepare the way for a brief account of the mission of *Malachi*. It is remarkable that there should be *no personal allusion* throughout the four chapters which compose this last book of the Old Testament, by which we should be able to refer it to any one author. The title, which is, of course, of later origin than the book itself, seems to be purposely ambiguous. We are left in doubt whether the name *Malachi* is to be taken as the name of a prophet, or refers to the nature of the message itself. "*Malachi*" may be a shortened form for *Malachijah* (cf. LXX.); "Angel of the Lord;" or it may be translated, "My angel." The title may, therefore, read, "The Book of the Word of the Lord to Israel by my angel," or, "by the angel of the Lord," or, "by the hand of Malachi" (the prophet). But it is well to bear in mind the remark made by Ewald that, seeing the very word "Malachi" is employed (chapter iii. 1) to denote the Divine messenger, "Behold, I will send my messenger," no prophet would have ventured to take such a name upon himself. Perhaps the book was named the "Book of the Angel," as containing the prediction; and then afterwards, when the early title was lost, it was supposed to be written by a prophet named *Malachi*. It has been attributed to Ezra himself, and to Nehemiah; but the authorship remains quite undecided. Internal evidence leads to the conclusion, that it was a message sent to the contemporaries of the two reformers; and that it was the last of the Jewish canon, because, after the time of Nehemiah, there would be great hesitation on the part of the Jews in adding to the Scriptures.

Casting a look over the pages, we are struck first with the element of condemnation and the threat of judgment which runs through them.

The priesthood is corrupt. The services of
the Temple are fallen into disorder. The whole
religious ceremonial has become a weariness and a
loathing. There is scepticism eating away the
heart of piety. Immorality is increasing in the
land. Domestic life is like a withered flower.
The "proud" are "called happy," and "they that
work wickedness are set up." Sorcery, adultery,
false swearing, oppression of the hireling in his
wages, the widow and the fatherless, and the turning aside of the stranger from his right. Such are
the flagrant sins which defile the land. And the
allusion, at the end of the book, to the alienation
of the children from their fathers, doubtless refers
to the sceptical, rationalistic, innovating spirit,
which broke out in such sayings as, "The table of
the Lord is contemptible." "Behold, what a
weariness is it!" "Every one that doeth evil is
good in the sight of the Lord, and He delighteth
in them." "Where is the God of judgment?"
"It is vain to serve God, and what profit is it that
we have kept His ordinance, and that we have
walked mournfully before the Lord of Hosts?"
We have not far to go to find the parallel of such
sayings. They are the scum of pride and irreligion
floating on the top of a great seething mass of
unbelief and worldliness in a time of transition;

such as was the time of Ezra, and such as is the time in which we live. With such a state of mind and manners to deal with, how did the prophetic voice appeal to the people?

The keynote is Love. "I have loved you, saith the Lord" (verse 2). The whole of the message comes out of this. What is their present state but an ungrateful rejection of Divine love, and dishonouring of the Divine covenant? It is but an unfolding of the original covenant of love that is set forth in the third chapter, as a bright glow of promise on the horizon of the true Israel. "Behold, I will send my messenger." "The Lord whom ye seek shall suddenly come to His Temple, even the messenger of the covenant, whom ye delight in: behold, He shall come, saith the Lord of Hosts" (iii. 1). There is something especially inspiring to the people in the promise that the same Angel of mercy who had been at the head of Israel all through the history of the past should reappear; and that to be their delight and their glory. True, it would be a terrible time for sinners. The *"day of His coming"* would *burn like fire.* The brightness of His face would purge their lives like "fullers' sope." But the subsequent purity and pleasantness was a prospect for all that feared the Lord and waited for Him to keep before them.

The spiritual renovation and revival would in-
augurate a period of general prosperity. "All
nations shall call you blessed : for ye shall be a
delightsome land, saith the Lord of Hosts."

Another striking feature in the book is the very
emphatic recognition of the *Church within the
Church,* of the germ of a *new Israel* in the midst
of the decay and rejection of the old. "Then they
that feared the Lord spake often one to another,
and the Lord hearkened and heard it : and a book
of remembrance was written before Him for them
that feared the Lord and that thought upon His
name. And they shall be Mine, saith the Lord of
Hosts, in that day when I make up My jewels, and
I will spare them, as a man spareth his own son
that serveth him. Then shall ye return, and dis-
cern between the righteous and the wicked, between him that serveth God and him that serveth
Him not" (iii. 16–18). This doctrine of a true
Israel, as distinguished from a merely fleshly Israel,
which was brought out so distinctly by the Apostle
Paul, in his Epistle to the Romans, was the con-
stant theme of the prophets : no doubt it was
nominally accepted by the people, but practically
it remained in abeyance until the time came when
it was conspicuously revealed in the ministry of
the Lord Jesus Christ.

We must also notice the *cosmopolitan tone* of this last book of the Old Testament. While the priests and Levites are rebuked for their neglect of the Mosaic Law, there is no Jewish exclusiveness in the Divine message. On the other hand, the rejection of the fallen Israel is made the opportunity for the proclamation of a universal gospel. "I have no pleasure in you, saith the Lord of Hosts, neither will I accept an offering at your hand. For from the rising of the sun, even unto the going down of the same, My name shall be great among the Gentiles; and in every place incense shall be offered unto My name and a pure offering: for My name shall be great among the heathen, saith the Lord of Hosts" (i. 10, 11). There seems to be an allusion to this breadth of the gospel of salvation in the prediction of the "*Day of the Lord,*" with which the book concludes. It is a *day of judgment* on the ungodly, which shall "*burn up the wicked like stubble;*" but it is not a mere day of destruction, it is the rising of "*the Sun of Righteousness*" into the heavens. There is "*healing in His wings.*" Surely those who read such a prediction would recall the language of the nineteenth Psalm, where the sun is described as lighting all the world: "His going forth is from the end of heaven, and his circuit unto the ends of

it : and there is nothing hid from the heat thereof." Some of the critics have made a great deal of
the parting admonition to "remember the Law of
Moses with the statutes and judgments," and the
prediction of the advent of Elijah; as though the
spirit of Malachi were merely that of *Levitical*
obedience and formalism. They have certainly
misapprehended the language. The meaning evidently is, that all true revival and restoration of
Israel must proceed along the lines of *faithfulness
to Jehovah and His covenant.* The children will
not be better than their fathers by despising and
trampling under foot the old things; but by
developing the germ which was in the old in the
new; putting "new wine into new wine-skins," but
getting the new wine out of the old vineyard.
Elijah was a great reformer; but he was followed
by *Elisha*, whose ministry extended over a much
larger sphere, and was much more beneficent. The
herald of the kingdom preached repentance; but
the Messiah Himself baptized with the Holy Ghost,
and sent forth His apostles to preach the Gospel
"to every creature." These, then, were the main
features of that last message, which, like a glow in
the evening sky, remained to keep alive the expectation of the rising day. The voice of a loving
Father addressed them. They were invited to put

away mere legalism and formalism, and live a spiritual life in fellowship with one another. They were pointed to the Temple, and bid to wait around it, in simple obedience and faith, until the Great Messiah should be revealed, and the Day of the Lord should come. We shall see, in the chapters which follow, how far this gracious appeal found a response among the Jewish people during those four long centuries when, amidst many and terrible trials, and much defection from the old standards, they still preserved the Sacred Scriptures which had been handed down to them and put in order by Ezra and his fellow-labourers, but when no new message directly from God was heard in their midst. It was a time of degeneracy and spiritual decay. But here and there, as we shall see, a gleam of light appeared upon the horizon.

CHAPTER II.

THE JEWISH PONTIFICATE.

THE Jewish Church, at the commencement of the fourth century before Christ, when the message of the last of the prophets, Malachi, was still fresh in their memory, held but few elements of spiritual growth and progress among them. The *Scriptures* were no doubt in common use, and their authority was clearly defined by the labours of Ezra, Nehemiah, and others of the religious leaders. The services of the Temple were restored, and for a time were punctually and carefully observed. The censures which were pronounced by the Prophet Malachi upon those who neglected the payment of tithes, who offered unworthy offerings, and who offended against the marriage laws, are evidence that the obligations of the law of Moses were publicly and universally recognised, and that the defections of the people from that law could not be excused either on the ground of their ignorance of what the law prescribed, or their doubt of its binding force. But there is no power in law alone to maintain the religious life of a people. The captives who returned from Babylon brought with them, in all probability, a very strong feeling of the necessity of repentance toward Jehovah, and of watchful care over their spiritual state in the future. For a hundred years a succession of eminent men, full of zeal for the law and a devout spirit, from Zerubbabel to Nehemiah, including many prophets, and some whose writings have come down to us, laboured to maintain the religious life of the new settlers in Palestine. But the external conditions of that life were very unfavourable. There was much disorder and confusion, which even the utmost patriotic efforts of the reformers were unable to remove. The spirit of the Persian rule, which under the great Cyrus had been protective towards the Jews, changed for the worse under his successor. The ambition which had sought for universal empire produced its usual pernicious fruits. Persia, under the weak-minded and vacillating Xerxes, hurled its forces against Eastern Europe under the leadership of Greece, was driven back with terrible loss and defeat, and sought to recover its prestige by attacks upon less formidable foes. The struggle for the complete subjection of Egypt went on for a considerable

B

period in a number of separate expeditions. Judea
suffered much by the passage of Persian armies
through it. As an instance of this we may mention that, between the years 377 B.C. and 374 B.C.,
there were two hundred thousand barbarian soldiers,
besides twenty thousand Greeks, in their neighbourhood, of course making requisitions upon them,
and otherwise burdening them ; at Acco were three
hundred ships of war, besides store ships ; and the
Persian army marched along the coast of Palestine
to Egypt. It must have been very difficult, under
such circumstances, to preserve anything like the
order and regularity of religious life. The institutions of the Jews fell into decay.

It was the policy of the Persian Empire, when
its central strength was waning, to depend more
and more on its representatives, in its various provinces or satrapies. The satrap, knowing himself
virtually a monarch, deputed his power to his
subordinates as his responsibility enlarged. The
Persian governor of Syria was no doubt compelled
to put more and more authority into the hands of
the Jewish high priest, who, though professedly a
religious ruler, soon became a kind of satrap within
his own domain. The people themselves looked to
him as their representative. And the high priest,
in his turn, used his religious position to exalt his

authority. The moral corruption which ensued we can easily understand when we remember the history of the Papacy during the Middle Ages. Josephus relates an instance which reveals a fearful state of things. On the death of the high priest Joiada, Bagoses, the Persian general, who was in the neighbourhood at the time, nominated Joshua as a successor; his brother John murdered him in the Temple, and left his dead body lying within the sacred precincts. Bagoses, hearing of the outrage, went in haste to Jerusalem, made his way into the sanctuary, and when the Jews exclaimed at his violation of the sanctity of the Temple, replied, "What, am I not as pure as the dead carcass of the murdered man which lies in your Temple?" He laid a heavy fine upon the nation, which was rigorously exacted for seven years.

The high priests were not only political despots, they were, by their dissensions and worldly ambition, corruptors of the people and of their institutions. It was the result of their irreligious spirit that the nation was led away into ruinous adventures. Such was the attempt made by some to support the Phœnicians of Tyre in their rebellion against the Persian power, which led the Persian king, Darius Ochus, to lay siege to Jericho to cap-

ture it, and carry off many of its inhabitants to
Egypt, sending others to Hyrcania to people it.
Jonathan, or John, the high priest, who murdered
his brother, still retained the high priesthood, and
continued in office until the year 340 B.C., when he
was succeeded by Jaddua, the high priest who met
Alexander the Great when he came to Jerusalem.
When the chief representative of a religion is corrupt, what can be expected? The high priest
Eliashib was rebuked by Nehemiah for his laxness
in carrying out reforms, which he rather hindered
than promoted; and his successors in the office for
nearly a century seem to have been worthless
characters. At the same time, the scene which
occurred on the advent of the great Macedonian
conqueror shows that the external pomp of worship, and the gorgeousness of the Temple rites,
were maintained. The solemn procession suddenly
emerged from the city: "The priestly tribe," says
Dean Stanley, "in their white robes; the high
priest, apparently the chief authority in the place,
in his purple and gold attire, his turban on his
head, bearing the golden plate on which was
inscribed the ineffable name of Jehovah." "'Who
are these?' said Alexander to the Samaritan
guides, who had gained from him the promise of
the destruction of the Temple, and the possession

of Mount Moriah. 'They are the rebels who deny
your authority,' said the rival sect. They marched
all night, in two ranks, preceded by torches, and
with the band of priestly musicians clashing their
cymbals. It was the sunrise of a winter morning
(December 21st), long afterwards observed as a
joyous festival, when they stood before the king.
To the astonishment of the surrounding chiefs,
Alexander descended from his chariot and bowed
to the earth before the Jewish leader. None ventured to ask the meaning of this seeming frenzy
save Parmenio alone. 'Why should he, whom
all men worship, worship the high priest of the
Jews?' 'Not him,' replied the king, 'but the
God, whose high priest he is, I worship. Long
ago, when at Dium in Macedonia, I saw in my
dreams such an one, in such an attire as this, who
urged me to undertake the conquest of Persia and
succeed!' Hand in hand with the high priest,
and with the priestly tribe running by his side, he
entered the sacred enclosure, and offered the usual
sacrifice; saw with pleasure the indication of the
rise of the Grecian power in the prophetic books;
granted free use of their ancestral laws, and specially, of the year of jubilee inaugurated so solemnly
a hundred years before under Nehemiah; promised
to befriend the Jewish settlements of Babylonia

and Media; and invited any who were disposed, to serve in his army, with the preservation of their sacred customs" ("Jewish Church," vol. iii. pp. 239, 240). There may be a large amount of exaggeration and fable in this account, which is taken from Josephus; but it is certain that the priestly authority was high enough at that time to be so influential for the people, and that the ceremonial system was largely maintained by the Jews. Indeed the fact that there was a rival temple set up by the Samaritans, on Mount Gerizim, would itself warrant the belief that the people of Jerusalem would be careful to exhibit their own ritual as superior to that of the sectarians.

Before referring to the indications which we are able to discover of surviving religious life among the Jews during this period of the high priesthood, it will be well to give some account of that rival worship which was set up by the Samaritans, which had important influence upon some of the religious views and practices of the Palestinian Jews for the next four hundred years. In the year 408 B.C. one Sanballat, chief of the Samaritans, obtained permission of the reigning Persian king, Darius Nothus, to build a temple on Mount Gerizim. His power over the king arose from the fact that he had furnished the Persian army with provisions on its way to Egypt. Manasseh, son of the high priest of Jerusalem, Joiada, was married to the daughter of Sanballat, and on that account was expelled by Nehemiah from Jerusalem (Neh. xiii. 28). He carried with him no very friendly feelings towards Judea. And it was through his influence that the rival worship was commenced. Josephus tells us that criminal and· disaffected Jews, from time to time, fled to Samaria and increased the number of the opposing sect. But the preponderating number of Jews preserved the Samaritans from idolatry. They worshipped Jehovah, though with imperfect rites and with a fragmentary Bible. Whether the Samaritan Pentateuch dates from this time, or from much later, cannot be certainly known. Ewald says, "At what time the temple on Gerizim was actually erected, and whether its construction was begun by Manasseh, with the powerful aid of Sanballat, we do not exactly know. It is true that even in the Persian times, and still more in the Greek, the Samaritans, like the Jews, certainly had their historians. In particular they possessed trustworthy records of the succession and fortunes of their chief priests, who, like the high priests in Jerusalem, constituted the only continuous links in their history. Special mention is made of a chief

priest named Hezekiah, who composed sacred
songs, and was still alive at the time of Alexander. But it is much to be regretted that the
only works which we now possess from the Samaritans, treating of their own ancient history, are
of very late date and extremely unsatisfactory.
So far as we can see from the traces which still
survive, a small sanctuary at any rate was in
existence on Gerizim before Alexander, chiefly
under the zealous interest of Manasseh of Jerusalem, whose name continued to be honoured
among the Samaritans for a long time afterwards
to a quite remarkable extent. A larger sanctuary,
for which fresh permission from the supreme government was requisite, in consequence of the necessary cost of building and the continuance of large
expenditure, was probably not erected there until
the Greek supremacy. It is undeniable that the
old city of Samaria was still the capital at the
time of Zerubbabel; but the greater fame which
Shechem very soon acquired could only have been
due to the temple on Gerizim" (vol. v., p. 220).
The temple of the Samaritans stood for about two
centuries. It was destroyed in 130 B.C. by the
high priestly ruler, John Hyrcanus I. (135–105
B.C.) The feeling of enmity against the Jews was
promoted by the building of the Samaritan temple;

and it found many occasions of violent expression in subsequent times down to the days of our Lord, when "*the Jews had no dealings with the Samaritans*" (John iv. 9). But it is due to this separation and enmity between the two peoples that the Samaritans preserved their copy of the Pentateuch, and that the Jews jealously guarded their own copy of the Law and boasted of its superior value. The special care which was taken of the writings of Moses extended to all the books of the Canon, and led to the growth of a school of learned men who devoted themselves to the preservation of the ancient Scriptures. But the Samaritan Pentateuch was the support of a false system of worship at Mount Gerizim, and in order to make it so the text was tampered with, while at the same time the Mosaic ritual was as far as possible preserved. The command, Deut. xxvii. 4, to set up the memorial stones at Mount Ebal, and to build there an altar to Jehovah, was changed in the Samaritan copy of the Pentateuch into a command to consecrate Mount Gerizim. Shechem had very special sanctity through its connection with the history of the patriarchs.

A recent writer, Dr. Edersheim, thus sums up the history of Samaria: " In 320 B.C. it passed from the rule of Syria to that of Egypt (Ptolemy

Lagi). Six years later it again became Syrian (Antigonus). Only three years afterwards, Ptolemy reconquered and held it for a very short time. On his retreat he destroyed the walls of Samaria and other towns. In 301 it passed again by treaty into the hands of Ptolemy; but in 298 it was once more ravaged by the son of Antigonus. After that it enjoyed a season of quiet under Egyptian rule, till the reign of Antiochus III., the Great, when it again passed temporarily, and under his successor Selenius IV. (Philopator), permanently, under Syrian dominion. In the troublous times of Antiochus IV. (Epiphanes) the Samaritans escaped the fate of the Jews by repudiating all connection with Israel, and dedicating their temple to Jupiter. In the contest between Syria and the Maccabees which followed, the Samaritans, as might be expected, took the part of the former."

After the destruction of the temple on Mount Gerizim, the city of Samaria was laid in ruins by the sons of Hyrcanus, and remained so for about a hundred years, until, under Gabinius, and subsequently under Herod, it was rebuilt, and renamed *Sebaste*, in honour of the Emperor Augustus. But notwithstanding all these vicissitudes in the external condition of the Samaritans, they seem to have preserved *some* remnants of religious life among them. In some of the Mosaic observances they were even stricter than the Jews themselves. At the time of our Saviour considerable change had taken place in the views and feelings of the Jews concerning them, and whereas at one time they were denounced as unclean, they were then acknowledged as admissible to the synagogue when they had given up their attachment to Mount Gerizim and estrangement from Jerusalem, and their food, which was once spoken of as swine's flesh in the sight of a Jew, was declared to be clean. It seems probable that among the remnants of the old Hebrew faith retained among them were the doctrine of the unity of God, angels and devils, and the resurrection of the dead. "They were most strict and zealous in what of Biblical or traditional law they received, and, most important of all, they looked for a Messiah in whom the promise would be fulfilled, that the Lord God would raise up a prophet from the midst of them, like unto Moses, in whom His words were to be, and unto whom they would hearken."

Now that a people so closely akin to the Jews should be at their doors for several hundred years, with an alien worship and a rival Scripture, had

an important effect upon the Jews themselves in
several particulars. It obliged them to look well
to the authority of their own religious rites, and
it promoted the study of the Scriptures and the
growth of the school of Scribes. It seems to be an
undoubted fact that after the restoration under
Ezra and Nehemiah there were many who wrote
books (cf. Eccles. xii. 12). The two Books of
Chronicles are a proof that historical literature
was cultivated. Commentaries and expositions
began to abound (see 2 Chron. xiii. 22, where
the story or commentary of the Prophet Iddo
refers to some later Scriptural writer). There is
a tradition preserved among the Rabbinical writings of a number of learned men who were called
the Great Synagogue, including among them Ezra
and Nehemiah ; and out of them came the body of
Scribes, whose " one aim was to promote reverence
for the Law, to make it the groundwork of the
people's life. They would write nothing of their
own, lest less worthy words should be raised on a
level with those of the oracles of God. If interpretation were needed, their teaching should be
oral only. No precepts should be perpetuated as
resting on their authority. In the words of later
Judaism they devoted themselves to the *Mikra*
(*i.e.* recitation, reading, as in Neh. viii. 8), the

careful study of the text, and laid down rules for
transcribing it with the most scrupulous precision
(cf. the Tract Sopherim in the Jerusalem Gemara)"
(Smith's Dict., Art. Scribes). It is a remarkable
fact that there is no writing, which has any claim
to be received as proceeding from the Jewish community as a religious book, for a hundred years
after the time of Ezra; a silence which no doubt
was the effect of the labours and principles of the
Scribes, and contributed much to the preservation
of the Scriptures in their purity. Towards the
end of the fourth century, however, and after the
Greek period had commenced, it seems possible
that one or two of the Apocryphal Books we now
possess appeared. Ewald goes so far as to place
both Baruch and Tobit in the fourth century. But
in this he is followed by very few critics. The
Books which were written after the rise of the
school of Scribes would undergo a very severe
scrutiny. It cannot be proved that any one of
those included in the Old Testament was written
after 400 B.C. That of Esther was probably the
work of Mordecai, and must have been composed
not later than 450 B.C. Possibly parts of the
Chronicles were as late as 400 B.C., though the
history itself breaks off with Cyrus. Ezra and
Nehemiah were written by the men whose names

they bear, and the Book of Malachi, as we have seen, was probably collected together before the death of Nehemiah.

The Book of Baruch is so evidently a mere imitation of the style of the prophets that it could not have been published during the generation which remembered Malachi. As, however, so great a critic as Ewald places it during the Persian period, a passing reference to it will help us to understand what was the kind of religious life which was maintained among the Jews of that time. We may divide the book into three portions :—

1. That which may be regarded as an original Hebrew composition, probably the work of some Jew in Babylon, following up the suggestions of the Prophet Jeremiah, that the people should submit themselves patiently to the Lord's hand. He has had before him the prophecies of Isaiah, Jeremiah, and Daniel, and the Book of Psalms, and has borrowed from them all, especially from Daniel. This portion extends from chapter i. 1 to chapter iii. 8.

2. The second part extends from iii. 8 to v. 9, and was written in Greek about the year 150 B.C. It is full of Alexandrian thought and language, and evidently was not a translation from an original in Hebrew.

3. The last portion is an epistle of Jeremiah, a spurious composition, dating about A.D. 100, added to the main book by some Christian writer.

The Hebrew portion, if not composed during the Babylonish captivity, may be assigned to the Persian period. In that case the recommendations to submission to the rule of the Babylonian monarch must be regarded as applying to the Persian power. But the objection to this is, that there would seem to be scarcely any reason for such admonitions, for the Persians did not oppress the returned captives, but rather favoured them. Ewald thinks the motive may have been to help the Jews to bear the exactions and confusions resulting from the wars between the Persians and the Egyptians. But this appears far-fetched and unnecessary. It is better to suppose that some original fragment came into the hands of the Greek translator, and that Baruch, if not the companion of Jeremiah, lived not very long after him, possibly at the court of Babylon. There is not, however, any great value in the few chapters which seem to be a relic of the captivity. They contain nothing more than confessions and prayers taken from the prophets. In so far as they point to a sense of sin and acknowledgment of Divine righteousness, they testify to real religious life. A collection of money is sent from the captive king of Judah and his nobles to Jerusalem, "And they said, Behold, we have sent you money to buy you burnt offerings, and sin offerings, and incense, and prepare ye incense, and offer upon the altar of the Lord our God : and pray for the life of Nebuchadnezzar, king of Babylon, and for the life of Belshazzar, his son, that their days may be upon earth as the days of heaven : and the Lord will give us strength, and lighten our eyes, and we shall live under the shadow of Nebuchadnezzar, king of Babylon, and under the shadow of Belshazzar, his son, and we shall serve them many days, and find favour in their sight" (chapter i. 10–12).

Now, there is no doubt that Jeremiah did recommend this peaceful submission to the king of Babylon, as we see in his 29th chapter. Ewald's theory is, that some late writer in the fourth century is writing as if Baruch, the companion and assistant of the prophet, were sent on a commission from his master to the captives, and indited a letter to the Holy Land in the cause of the captive people. He thinks that it was written at the time of dangerous risings against the Persians. But such risings were quite local in their character, and not of sufficient importance to account for the origin of the book. Moreover, the very distinct separation of the latter part from the former makes it impossible to sustain the theory. Professor J. J. Kneucker, in his very learned work published in 1879, has gone very thoroughly into the critical question as to the authenticity and antiquity of the Book of Baruch, and comes to the conclusion that it proceeded from the Pharisaic school after the destruction of Jerusalem, and that it aimed at the revival of Jewish feeling under the Roman supremacy. But while this view is widely separated from Ewald's, it seems scarcely tenable. The small portion which harmonises with the spirit of the ancient prophets, if it be a genuine relic of the Captivity, must have served to keep alive in the Jewish Church feelings of penitence, and hope in the future glory of Israel. "O Lord Almighty, God of Israel, the soul in anguish, the troubled spirit crieth unto Thee. Hear, O Lord, and have mercy; for Thou art merciful: and have pity upon us, because we have sinned before Thee. For Thou endurest for ever, and we perish utterly" (chapter iii. 1-3). And the promise is repeated, " I will bring them again into the land which I promised with an oath unto their fathers, Abraham, Isaac, and Jacob, and they shall be lords of it, and I will increase them, and they shall not be diminished. And I will make an everlasting covenant with them to be their God, and

C

they shall be my people ; and I will no more drive
my people of Israel out of the land that I have
given them " (chapter ii. 34, 35).

On the whole it is impossible to attach any importance to the book. It was not noticed among
the early fathers of the Christian Church. And
when it was quoted, as it was by the writers of
the third century, it was taken to be the genuine
work of Jeremiah. It cannot be said to break the
silence of the fourth century B.C. We are left to
face the fact, that after the time of Malachi no
Scripture was produced, nor was the religious state
of the people such as would suggest the likelihood
of any writing being added to the sacred rolls. As
we shall see in subsequent chapters, the formality
which increased with the spiritual decline of the
nation became itself a preservative against the
multiplication of sacred books. The sense of a
departed inspiration, as it became deeper in the
course of time, "hedged about the law" with a
rampart of superstitious reverence. Such reverence promoted the work of transcription. The
law which authorised the Temple-worship at Jerusalem had to be maintained ; and the same class of
learned men who employed themselves in searching
the Scriptures for the support of the priesthood,
devoted themselves to the preservation of the

historical and prophetic writings, which came to be held in a respect only a little lower than that which surrounded the Pentateuch. The practical discipline which the Jews received during the time of their captivity, and for a long period after their restoration, must have raised in their estimation the value of those Books of Scripture which spoke to them of their future. This we can see from the fact that the Samaritans, who were not in sympathy with such prospects, did not appreciate the prophets, and retained only the Books of Moses. It was probably during the Persian period that the learned Jews fully recognised the necessity of closing their Canon; and the tradition which tells us of "the Great Synagogue," to whose labours the completion of the Canon was due, gives the date of *Simon the Just* soon after the commencement of the Grecian period (310–290 B.C.), as the last date in connection with that important body which is said to have continued for two centuries. It has been observed by Canon Westcott that there is no sound authority for the belief that any book was added to the Old Testament between the time of Malachi and that of Christ. The Greek Books which constitute the Apocrypha were no doubt added to the Septuagint at a very late period.

CHAPTER III.

THE COURT OF THE GENTILES.

THERE are periods in the history of nations which seem to be blanks ; when there is little or nothing to record, or when a state of external disorder and confusion has clouded the atmosphere of the national life to so great an extent that no clear outlines of historical delineation can be discerned. It has already been remarked that the century which followed the close of the Scripture canon, from about .420 B.C. to 320 B.C., must be described as one of stagnation and decay in the history of the Jewish Church. The rule of the high priests was maintained, but it was a mere preservation of the old in its formal completeness, not a development of its vital elements ·in new growth and higher instruction. There was, we are told, "*a certain uniform culture of religion and morals*" in the nation generally. But that did not hinder the process of corruption in the higher classes. Neither was the spirit of the people roused

by any messenger who appealed to its national vocation or rebuked its slothful lethargy. The State,
which had been restored by the remarkable favour
of the Persian monarchy, was in considerable danger when the Persian Empire was broken up into
satrapies, and threatened by the rising power of
Greece. The New Jerusalem, which had been
erected round the new Temple, depended upon
the maintenance of the priesthood. And the
priests knew their power, and took care that the
people should feel it. But Divine Providence
ordained a course of external events which won-
derfully changed the spiritual history of the Jewish
people.

The *Greek* period, as it is generally called, which
might be said to begin with the defeat of Xerxes
by the Greeks, in the middle of the fifth century,
and which culminated in the conquest of Syria by
Alexander the Great in 333 B.C., brought about
most radical changes in the Jewish Church; and
it is of the utmost importance that these changes
should be thoroughly examined and understood
in order to appreciate the subsequent appearance
of new lights, or what claimed to be so, on the
horizon. The great military monarchies of Asia
were under the necessity, in order to maintain
their prestige, to undertake from time to time

some great enterprise of conquest. The Persian
kingdom in 480 B.C. was driven by the force of
circumstances to lead its armies towards the west.
Egypt had succumbed to its sword. India on the
east had been conquered. Thrace and Macedonia
had vainly resisted its progress. It remained
to descend from the higher and more moun-
tainous regions, to the fruitful plains and well-
watered fields of Greece. An immense multitude
of soldiers was collected together, and a large
and well-appointed fleet. But both availed nothing against the heroism and intellectual force
of that extraordinary people, whose rapid development within the small territory of the Greek
coasts and Peloponnesus is one of the wonders
of the world. For a hundred years after the
defeat and retirement of Xerxes the Persian
monarchs sought to recover their military power ;
partly by corrupting Greek statesmen, and taking
advantage of the internal troubles of Greece, and
partly by expeditions against revolting satraps.
But the end could not be far off, and it was
brought about by that extraordinary man *Alexander the Great,* who burned to revenge the
ancient dishonour of his Macedonian fatherland
by the conquest of its enemy. A weak prince
was seated on the Persian throne, Darius III.

Alexander was a mere youth when he crossed the Hellespont and invaded Asia Minor in the spring of 334 B.C. Darius despised the young man's inexperience, and left the extremities of his empire unguarded. The battle of Granîcus, in the neighbourhood of Sardis, opened the eyes of the careless and weak-minded Persian. All Asia Minor lay at the feet of the Macedonian conqueror. Persia was compelled to act on the defensive, while Alexander marched rapidly and without opposition towards Babylonia. Two great battles, *Issus* and *Arbela*—the one, as it were, at the gate of the Persian stronghold, and the other in the very chosen spot of Persia, the Plains of Adiabene—brought the conflict to an end in the utter overthrow of the Eastern despotism. All Syria then submitted to Alexander. Damascus, Tyre, Sidon fell into his hands, and he became the prominent figure of the world. That he was a cruel man there can be no doubt at all, as we see in the fulfilment of the prophecy of Zechariah in the siege and destruction of Gaza (ix. 5); but he was not without his better impulses, and the influence on his mind of his great teacher, the philosopher Aristotle, may have prepared him to deal somewhat more considerately with a people so remarkable, and so famed for wisdom and virtue, as the Jews. Josephus in his work, "Against Apion" (i. 22), refers to the conferences which Aristotle is said to have had with a learned and philosophical Jew, as related by Clearchus, one of Aristotle's disciples. It is impossible to determine whether there is any truth in this story or not. But it is certain that Aristotle, before he became the tutor of Alexander, was in Mysia, and married there a relative of the King of Atarnea, at whose court he is said to have found the Jewish teacher. There is no difficulty, therefore, in accounting for the origin of the story. The one consideration which weighs against its credibility is the carelessness of Josephus and his evident desire to glorify his nation. The conduct of Alexander, however, certainly requires explanation. He was wounded at the siege of Gaza, and was no doubt greatly enraged against that city for its stubborn defence. In his cruel passion he put ten thousand citizens to death, and sold the rest as slaves, with the women and children. It is said that he put the commander to death in the most barbarous fashion, fastening his feet to his chariot by thongs thrust through the soles, and dragging "him round the city with swift horses." We learn from Josephus that an order of submission was sent to Jerusalem and received by Jaddua, the high priest. The answer was, that the oath which the Jewish nation had sworn, to serve Darius, King of Persia, could not be violated. And Alexander raved with passion, and threatened Jerusalem with destruction. This was before his subjugation of Tyre and Gaza, and the circumstances attending the prolonged resistance of these cities would certainly not tend to allay the irritation of the young and impetuous general, before whom a whole empire had fallen. We have already referred to the extraordinary change which took place in Alexander's feelings and conduct when he arrived at Jerusalem. Whether the account of his dream and its fulfilment in the appearance of Jaddua with his procession of priests be a fabrication or not, we have to face the fact that not only did Alexander spare the city, but from that time favoured the Jews in the most remarkable manner. It is said that certain predictions in the Jewish Scriptures were shown to him, and that they made a great impression on his mind. These were the predictions in Daniel vii. 6 ; viii. 1–7, 21 ; xi. 3 ; and that in Zech. ix. 1–8, concerning the cities which he had just subdued. The Jews were freed from tribute in the Sabbatical year ; they were to have entire liberty to follow out their own religious

institutions and laws; and it is said that at the
same time Alexander invited the Jews, as many as
pleased, to join his army with the same indul-
gences, which invitation was accepted, according
to the testimony of Hecatæus, as recorded by
Josephus. Such treatment is an indication that
the Jews were regarded as an exceptional people.
Alexander was himself full of intelligence, and he
may have discerned an elevation of mind and character among the Jews which led to his milder
dealings with them. At all events, it is an indis-
putable fact that from the time of Alexander's
visit to Jerusalem, 332 B.C., commenced a new
period in the national history. They continued
for more than a century to be favoured by rulers
and princes, and their intellectual qualities were
rapidly developed under the fostering influence of
the Ptolemies, so that they rose in some of their
Egyptian representatives to the highest eminence
as thinkers and scholars.

It has been remarked by Ewald that Alexander
was himself a type in his own person of the character of the Greco-Macedonian empire. There was
great intensity and marvellous daring, but little
steadfastness and permanence, and fearful corruption. The conquests of Alexander were like the
raging of a sudden storm, which " convulsed all

the kingdoms to their very depths, and hurled them against one another, and if they were not instantly dashed to pieces, roused them violently to assume new forms." " In Israel, also, at once so old and so young, far more violent changes were speedily produced by this storm and its after-effects, than by the Persian supremacy. On the soil of its ancient fatherland it had again acquired sufficient strength and firmness to take a more active part in the mighty efforts and new destinies of the world. The past had secured to it enough preparatory culture, and recent vicissitudes had sufficiently excited and strained its attention, to prevent it from remaining unaffected by the peculiar characteristic of the Greek spirit, to render it susceptible to the powerful attractions of its charm, and to enable it speedily to rival it in everything. When the Israelite and the Greek were first brought into contact, it was inevitable that the union and fusion of the two should appear easy. Israel had saved enough from the high culture of its ancient days. Activity of mind and a readiness to learn were common to both nations; and there were, in addition, many reasons why the greater purity of morals, for which Israel was distinguished among many Asiatic nations, could be nothing but acceptable to the Greek ruler. But the growing fusion only brought the deeper-seated antagonisms between the nationalities and religions on either side into sharper collision. In breaking, therefore, the heavy shell which still covered Israel, and bringing in the largest amount of activity and freedom possible at the time, the Greek age forced the whole spirit which prevailed during that period of the history into the most violent labour and an attitude of the most energetic decision" (vol. v., pp. 223-4).

One of the most influential of Alexander's wars was that which he carried on in Egypt; and one of the most remarkable events of that Egyptian career was the selection of a new harbour, opposite the island of Pharos, and the order which was given for a city to be built there and named *Alexandria*. This was in the same year with his visit to Jerusalem, 332 B.C., and before his final victories over Persia. The death of the great Macedonian took place at the city of Babylon, in the spring of 323 B.C., chiefly through his own debaucheries. His body was embalmed, and after two years carried to Egypt, where it was interred, first at Memphis, and subsequently in his new city of Alexandria. His new and rapidly conquered empire had yet to be consolidated, and for this purpose it was divided among his generals and minis-

ters by Perdiccas, the regent of Macedonia. The
name of *Ptolemy Lagus*, to whom Egypt was
assigned, is associated for some years to come with
the Jewish people; for several provinces were
speedily subjugated by the Egyptian ruler, Judea,
Samaria, Phœnicia, and Cœlo-Syria, and it is said
that Ptolemy went himself to Jerusalem for the
purpose of sacrificing in the Temple, and declared
himself master of the country. One form of the
story is, that he took advantage of the Sabbath, on
which he knew that the Jews would make no
resistance, and seized the city without striking a
blow. Many thousands of Jews were on this
occasion taken from Judea to Egypt, and many
others followed them voluntarily, so that Egypt
soon became flocked with them. They manned the
garrison; they formed part of the army; and they
were settled with special privileges in Alexandria,
being placed on an equality with the Macedonians
there, so that they had much to do with the first
formation of that new commercial centre, where,
we may be sure, their remarkable business capacities
would find abundant scope as the advantages of the
city were developed. Josephus refers to letters of
Alexander and Ptolemy which were extant in his
time, and to the testimony of the writings of
Hecatæus, which, however, are now lost to us.

It will be necessary, before we proceed with this account of the Jewish religion, to estimate the in- influence of Alexandria upon the nation; for the migration which took place was so large and long continued that, from the beginning of the third century B.C., it may be said there were *two* Jewish nations, one in Judea and the other in Egypt. It was little more than the project of a commercial centre at Alexandria which was due to the genius and insight of the great conqueror himself. The realisation of that project was the work of a man whose greatness rivalled that of Alexander. Ptolemy I. was the son of Lagus, a mere Greek adventurer, and his mother was a woman of low repute, but at the Court of Philip of Macedon he rose to eminence, as the intimate friend of the heir to the throne and an able soldier. A clear-minded, acute, and powerful intellect, thoroughly Greek in its character, was united in him with all the energy and determination of a great general. His advice it was that led to the partition of the Macedonian empire, and his shrewdness which selected Egypt for himself. But he was no mere worshipper of material wealth. He aimed at the highest ends; the promotion of the prosperity of his subjects through their intellectual and moral elevation. "Mind was the secret of Greek power;

for that Ptolemy would work. He would have an aristocracy of intellect; he would gather round him the wise men of the world, and he would develop to the highest the conception of Philip when he made Aristotle the tutor of his son Alexander. The consequences of that attempt were written in letters of blood over half the world. Ptolemy would attempt it once more with gentler results. For though he fought long, and often, and well, as despot of Egypt, no less than as general of Alexander, he was not at heart a man of blood, and made peace the end of all his wars" (Kingsley, "Alexandria and her Schools," page 14). In carrying out the ideas of the conqueror, Ptolemy resolved that Alexandria should not only be a metropolis of trade, but of learning as well. According to his lights he revived religion, and founded the celebrated Alexandrian Library and Museum. This latter was of much importance, as the collection of books in it was a gathering-place of the learned under the protection of the ruler, and it was erected close to the royal palace. It was a vast building with porticoes, where the great scholars could meet and converse; lecture - rooms where they could address audiences; a banqueting-hall where they could enjoy festivity and put forth their witty sallies; and a staff of teachers

supported at the royal expense, together with
collections of curiosities and botanical and zoo-
logical gardens.   Hence arose very rapidly into
existence and working the celebrated Alexandria
School, numbering among its scholars eminent
mathematicians, artists, and metaphysicians, and
men of culture in almost all departments of
knowledge.

The city of Alexandria was divided into three
regions: one of which was named the Jewish
Quarter (Regio Judæorum), the others Brucheium
and Rhacotis, that is, the Greek Quarter and the
Egyptian Quarter.   The number of the Jews it is
very difficult to estimate with any certainty, but
in the time of Philo, that is, shortly before the
Christian era, they were reckoned at one million,
and are said to have formed two-fifths of the
population.   It was the policy of Ptolemy to
favour the Jews.   They were not only granted civil
privileges, but we can have little doubt that some
of their learned men were admitted into the
highest circle of the Alexandrian University,
where their Jewish wisdom would have full scope
to influence the Greek mind, just as, on the other
hand, the Greek Philosophy and Science would, in
turn, modify the views of Jewish teachers.   We
must here refer to the writings of Hecatæus of

Abdêra, who is said to have published a work giving an account of the Jews during the reign of Ptolemy. The reality and genuineness of this work, which has not come down to us, has been doubted. (See Origen against Celsus (i.) and Eichhorn's "Bibliothek"). But the time of its appearance was favourable to the production of such a book, and there seems no improbability in its being written by a Greek. Josephus stands up boldly for its authority. In this work it is said there was an account of a certain chief priest of the Jews, named Hezekiah, who went voluntarily to Egypt at the time when Ptolemy invited them to enter his service. He was sixty years old, and much respected among his own people; learned and eloquent, and skilful in business. "This venerable man became acquainted with us, and he read to some of his friends a description of the peculiarities of his nation, for he had with him a written account of their institutions and civil polity." We may add to this reference to Hezekiah the testimony which Hecatæus bears to the steadfastness and purity of the Jews and their superiority to superstitions which prevailed at that time. The following singular incidents will illustrate the general tone of his remarks :—" As I was once travelling by the Red Sea, there was one among

D

the horsemen who attended us named Masollam, a
brave and strong man, and according to the testimony of all the Greeks and barbarians, a very skilful archer.   Now when the whole multitude was on
the way, an augur called out to them to stand still,
and this man inquired the reason of their halting.
The augur showed him a bird, and told him that if
that bird remained where he was, it would be
better for them all to remain ; if he flew on, they
might proceed ; but if he flew back, they must
return.   The Jew said nothing, but bent his bow
and shot the bird to the ground.   This act
offended the augur and some others, and they
began to utter imprecations against the Jew,
but he replied, ʻWhy are you so foolish as to
take care of this unfortunate bird ?   How could
this fowl give us any wise directions respect-
ing our journey, when he could not save his own
life ?   Had he known anything of futurity, he
surely would not have come here to be killed by
the arrow of Masollam the Jew ʼ ” (Jos., Ag. Ap.
i. 22).   “ Wherever the Jews went,” says Ewald,
“ they carried with them their ancestral faith,
and the peculiarly tenacious and inflexible pride
which was so closely knit with it.   They were
conscious of being raised above the thousand forms
of heathen superstition, and accordingly felt them-

selves everywhere impelled, among the heathen, to
maintain or aspire after a certain elevation of life ;
especially when they came to be sought for by so
many potentates of the time. When the Jews
serving in Alexander's army were set in Babylon
to assist in restoring the temple of Belus, they
obstinately refused ; and those who lived in Palestine destroyed all the altars which the first
Macedonians tried to erect in their country."

The two motives which wrought in the minds of
the Jewish emigrants, to maintain their religion,
and yet promote their influence and prosperity
among the strange people with whom they mingled,
led them to strive jealously for privileges and
position, so that they secured to themselves a
large degree of power. "In every city they endeavoured to secure a magistracy of their own,
to form an exclusive community, not merely for
their religious duties, but even for everything
relating to taxes and property, so as to have all
their internal disputes, whether about sacred or
civil matters, adjusted within their own limits.
In each town of any size, accordingly, they constituted a *Politeuma*, *i.e.* an organised community
with a large body of *gerontes* (senators), a small
number of *archons* (executive officers), and a chief,
who, in a country of importance, might even bear

the title and dignity of an *ethnarch*, or national prince ; in Alexandria he was generally designated *alabarch*.   This struggle on the part of the Jews resident among the heathen, for higher respect, liberty and independence, was so vigorous, and the air of the Greek age so mild, that even those who had been at first transported as prisoners or slaves almost everywhere regained their freedom, just as at a later day the community of Rome was formed chiefly out of the *liberti* settled on the other bank of the Tiber."

There can be no doubt that while the Jews thus maintained a very independent position in Egypt and elsewhere among the heathen, they kept up for a considerable period very closely their connection with Jerusalem.   This they did by regularly contributing to the support of the Temple, and by the synagogue worship, which helped them to realise their brotherhood and nationality.   But it was not possible for so great a force as that which was represented in the Greek mind and spirit to be brought into contact with the Jews without greatly modifying their religious character. This we shall show in subsequent chapters ; but meanwhile we must call the reader's attention to the fact that hitherto, while the Jews possessed in their sacred books treasures of wisdom and knowledge given them directly by the Divine Spirit, which lifted them both morally and spiritually high above heathen nations, they had been very little under the influence of great philosophical minds; indeed, philosophy strictly so-called was unknown among them. At Alexandria there were two main currents of intellectual influence, the mathematical and the metaphysical, which began to bear upon the Jewish teachers very decidedly from the time of Ptolemy Philadelphus, the successor of Ptolemy I. The Greek version of the Old Testament was made by the command of the Egyptian monarch. But it would be a misrepresentation to say, that the one sole ground of that command was to gratify the curiosity of the Greek and Egyptian population. The Jewish Rabbis who were employed in the translation were as truly under the influence of the Greek spirit, as the Greeks, for whom the translation was made, were under the influence of Jewish teaching. The subsequent history of the Alexandrian school of Jewish writers clearly shows that there was an intermingling of Greek philosophy and Hebrew doctrine, which produced a very strange result in a mystical theology as decidedly distinct from the teaching of the Old Testament as it was from the spirit of the old Grecian sages.

But before we proceed to describe more fully the effects of Alexandrian scholasticism and philosophy on the Jewish Church, we must glance at the other side of the picture, and describe one prominent figure which remains identified with the old Jewish spirit still surviving at Jerusalem, and in the Palestinian branch of the nation. In 300 B.C. the high priest Onias died, and he was succeeded by his son *Simon*, who is generally known as *Simon the Just.* A few words with regard to his character and work will help us to understand the religious state of the Jews during that long period of rest and external prosperity which they enjoyed under the early Ptolemies and the Egyptian rule. In the Book of Ecclesiasticus (chapter l.) we find a description of this remarkable man, which will show how he was regarded by the Jews about a hundred years after his death. " How was he honoured in the midst of the people on his coming out of the sanctuary? He was as the morning star in the midst of a cloud, and as the moon at the full : as the sun shining upon the temple of the Most High, and as the rainbow giving light in the bright clouds; and as the flower of roses in the spring of the year, as lilies by the rivers of waters, and as the branches of the frankincense-tree in the time of

summer : as fire and incense in the censer, or as
a vessel of beaten gold set with all manner of
precious stones, and as a fine olive-tree budding
forth fruit, and as a cypress-tree which groweth
up to the clouds. When he put on the robe
of honour, and was clothed with the perfection
of glory, when he went up to the holy altar, he
made the garment of holiness honourable." This
is evidently an ideal description from the point
of view of the most extreme ritualism. Simon is
regarded as the ideal high priest, and his appearance is celebrated as the perfection of high priestly
splendour, and therefore as the central figure of
a perfect Temple service. It is said in the Rabbinical traditions that an angel appeared to Simon
every year during his Pontificate. The spirit of
his rule is well represented in the threefold saying
which is represented as the legacy of the Great
Synagogue, or Assembly of Jewish Divines, to
their successors : " Be careful in judgments, set
up many *Talmidim* (*i.e.* learned students), and
make a hedge about the *Thorah* (law)." On three
things, Simon said, the permanence of the world,
that is of the Jewish world, depends ; on the
Thorah (faithfulness to the law and its pursuit) ;
on worship (the non-participation in Grecianism,
i.e. strict Judaism) ; and in works of righteous-

ness. It is difficult to determine the exact time
when Simon lived, that is, whether the title
Simon the Just is to be referred to the first Simon
or the second Simon ; but it is of little consequence to settle the controversy, as the general
fact remains the same, that there was, about the
commencement of the third century, or a little
later, a great reformer and spiritual leader, who
did his best to restore the material structure of
the Temple and its internal splendour, and to
revive among the people the devout observance
of the law.

"All the traditions combine in representing
Simon as closing the better days of Judaism.
Down to his time it was always the right hand
of the high priest that drew the lot of the consecrated goats ; and after his time the left and
right wavered and varied. Down to his time the
red thread round the neck of the scapegoat turned
white, as a sign that the sins of the people were
forgiven ; afterwards its change was quite uncertain. The candlestick at the entrance of the
Temple burned, in his time, without fail ; afterwards it often went out. Two faggots a day
sufficed to keep the flame on the altar alive in his
time ; afterwards piles of wood were insufficient.
In his last year he was said to have foretold his

death, from the omen that whereas on all former
occasions he was accompanied into the Holy of
Holies on the Day of Atonement, to the entrance
only, by an old man clothed in white from head
to foot; in that year his companion was attired
in black, and followed him as he went in and came
out.   These were the forms in which the later
Jewish belief expressed the sentiment of his tran-
scendent worth, and of the manifold changes which
were to follow him" (Stanley, vol. iii., p. 248).
There was some remnant in Simon of the old
reverence for purity of heart and life.   There was
a gentle spirit in him, which is preserved in some
of the traditions concerning him.   He is said to
have hated the severe asceticism of the Nazarites,
and when a young man came to be consecrated,
he reluctantly yielded to his request to remove
all personal attractions, until he found that the
vow was the true offering of his heart, when he
" embraced his brow, and exclaimed, ' Would that
there were many such Nazarites in Israel.' "

No doubt there are some signs of regretful remembrance of a departed glory in the traditional
Simon.   He represents the people's sense of their
own degeneracy.   But the mere worship of a great
name has little influence in arresting spiritual decline.   Rabbinism took the place of devout study

of the Old Testament. Mere slavish Ritualism
cast out spiritual life. "Israel made void the law
by its traditions. Under a load of outward ordinances and observances its spirit had been crushed.
The religion as well as the grand hope of the Old
Testament had become externalised" (Edersheim).
Palestine, while it still held fast to the letter of
the law, and, therefore, rendered a great service
to the cause of religion by handing on the Scriptures, sank both intellectually and morally to a
lower level. It was at this time that another
form of Judaism appeared in Egypt, distinguished
both by its intellectual form and moral breadth,
and thither our attention must be carried awhile.

CHAPTER IV.

THE SEPTUAGINT.

IT has often been observed that the connection of the Bible with history supplies one of the most convincing evidences of the Divine authority of the written Word. There is nothing in the whole course of the Jewish annals more remarkable than the series of events which led to the preparation of the Greek version of the Old Testament. What that work has accomplished in the diffusion of revealed truth through the world no human mind can ever estimate. How the way of the Lord was prepared by it, how it laid the foundations on which Christianity itself built up its higher and fuller communications, we can never perfectly describe, although the fact that it to a large extent superseded the Hebrew Bible, and was for a considerable period the sacred volume of the Christian Church, must be sufficient to show that it was a chosen instrument of Divine providence in the work of human salvation. Everything which throws light on the earliest history of the Septuagint must therefore be of value in looking forward, as we do, in studying the history of the Jewish Church, to the appearance of the Universal Religion, the one " *Word of God*," which shall break down the "*middle wall of partition*" between Jew and Gentile, and "*make one new man, so making peace.*"

We have already noticed the singular providence in the favour shown towards the Jews, both by the Persian monarchs and by the Macedonian. Whether the mind of Alexander the Great was influenced by his great teacher Aristotle, as the result of intercourse with learned Jews, or whether special Divine communications were sent to the young conqueror, as he is said to have intimated when he visited Jerusalem, it is impossible now to say. It is certain that Alexander treated the Jews with great indulgence, and that his policy was followed by the Ptolemies of Egypt, who for a very long period had possession of Palestine. Ptolemy Lagi, in 320 B.C., sent his general, Nicanor, to subdue Judea, Samaria, Phœnicia, and Cœlo-Syria. After a short war Laomedon, the general of the Syrian monarch Antiochus, was driven out, and the people were glad to exchange a time of war and uncertainty for the rule of a

benevolent prince. We are informed by Josephus
that on this occasion Jerusalem was again visited
by a conqueror, and Ptolemy is said to have sacri-
ficed in the Temple after the example of the Macedonian conqueror, Alexander. It is also stated
by Agatharchides that the possession of Jerusalem
was the result of a stratagem, the Egyptian ruler
entering the city on the Jewish Sabbath, when it
was not lawful for the people to resist his entrance
by force of arms. But there was doubtless little
inclination on the part of the Jews to oppose one
who was evidently so well disposed to protect
them. Many Jews and many Samaritans were
taken prisoners and carried to Egypt at this time.
But, though nominally slaves, they were very soon
liberated and employed by Ptolemy in defence of
his garrisons. Some were sent to Cyrene. Some
were located in the neighbourhood of Alexandria,
privileges being granted them similar to those
granted by Alexander the Great to Macedonian
settlers.

It is not wonderful that after this time many
Jews emigrated from Palestine, and shared in
those remarkable regulations by which they were
provided with a new sphere of ambition and a
prospect of great influence and prosperity. Josephus informs us that letters were extant in his

time, both of Alexander and Ptolemy, confirming
these facts, which are also described by Hecatæus
—although we are not able to prove that the so-
called history of Hecatæus was genuine. There
was no part of the world where the Jews congre-
gated in such large numbers as at Alexandria,
where they are said to have been almost half the
population, and in the time of our Lord numbered
one million. As we might naturally suppose, they
soon came under the influence of Greek thought
and culture, although they gave as much as they
received. They preserved their strict separation
from the heathen in the forms of their worship.
They had in Egypt their prayer-houses or synagogues, and they diligently studied their law,
maintaining their contribution to the support of
the central seat of their religion in the Temple
at Jerusalem. "The close connection established
between the Hagiocracy and a school of trained
interpretation of the Bible and teaching of the law,
which from the time of Ezra had its principal seat
in Jerusalem, rendered this the sacred centre from
which all the minuter ordinances and decisions
of religious duty were constantly issued into all
heathen countries ; and this bond of union was
necessarily tightened, and a stricter watch kept
over the remotest Jews, to counteract the danger

to which every Jewish element was exposed, of evaporating when it was so widely dispersed. Thus, in a certain sense, there now arrived an age when, as one of the most ancient prophets had fore-told, the 'law and justice' of the true God went forth from the hill of Zion into all the world, and the pilgrimages of foreign Jews to the feasts at Jerusalem, which were evidently regarded with great favour and promoted by the priests, afforded on a small scale a prelude to the universal dominion of this religion over the whole world" (Ewald, v. 244).

But there very soon arose among the prosper-ous Jews of Alexandria a school of cultured and thoughtful men, whose minds had been brought into contact with the best results of heathen philo-sophy; and the translation of the Hebrew Scrip-tures into Greek was in some measure, no doubt, the work of this school, or at least went on side by side with its growth. We must now relate the circumstances which led to the formation of a Greek Bible, the fruit of centuries and the joint product of many hands, but the initiation of which can certainly be dated in the earliest years of the Ptolemaic period.

One of the most remarkable men of the fourth century B.C. was the Athenian *Demetrius Pha-*

lereus. He had governed the city of Athens for
ten years under Cassander of Macedonia with so
much moderation, wisdom, and humanity, that he
was worshipped by the people. In Athens, it is
said, there were as many statues erected to Demetrius as there were days in the year. It was the
policy, however, of. Cassander's great rival and
enemy, Antigonus, to give autonomy to the cities
of Greece in order to detach them from the opposite cause. Demetrius Poliorcetes was sent to
Athens in 307 B.C. to proclaim this new liberty to
Athens. Finding Demetrius Phalereus there he
immediately banished him. His statues were de-
molished, and the materials of which they were
made were used to form various vessels of a meaner
sort. Demetrius fled to Cassander, but his protector soon died, and he then betook himself to
Egypt, and placed himself at the disposal of
Ptolemy I., who had a quick eye for merit, and
knew how to gather round him those who would
be his efficient helpers in the raising of a new and
powerful state. Demetrius was one of the most
learned men of antiquity, and the influence of his
Alexandrian activity may be said to have extended
itself over the whole world. It was he who suggested to Ptolemy the founding of the museum and
the great library connected with it, and he be-

came the president of the new school which may be
dated from that time, in which many of the most
eminent men of the world were gathered together.
It seems not unlikely that Demetrius suggested to
Ptolemy Lagi that a Greek translation of the law
of Moses should be placed in the Library. But
this cannot be ascertained. There is no improbability, however, in what is stated by Aristeas, that
Ptolemy II., *Philadelphus*, who certainly commenced the work of the Septuagint, was led to do
so by the persuasion and under the direction of
Demetrius. In 285 B.C. Ptolemy Lagi abdicated
in favour of his son. Demetrius did not approve
of this step, and after the death of the old king
in 284 B.C., *Philadelphus* banished the man who
opposed his accession. He died in prison, it is
said, by the bite of an asp. Archbishop Usher
ascribes the work of translation of the Pentateuch
into Greek to the year 277, the eighth year of
Philadelphus, but he does so on the authority of
Aristeas, whose account has indeed been followed,
until comparatively modern times, with implicit
reliance, but is now universally discarded as a mass
of fables. The chief particulars, however, of the
story, which is now familiar to most, must be
briefly recounted for the sake of the better dis-
crimination of the true from the false.

E

Aristeas was one of the officers of the guards in
the army of King Ptolemy II. He and Sosibius of
Tarentum, and Andreas, one of the nobles of the
court, being much interested in the Jews, when
they heard of the project of Demetrius, and the
commission given him by the king to procure a
Greek version of the Hebrew law, took occasion
to plead for the liberty of the Jewish slaves, who
were at that time very numerous in Egypt. Their
motive, they explained, was that the people of the
Jews might be the more disposed to assist the
king. It is said that Ptolemy was persuaded, and
not only ordered the slaves to be manumitted, but
paid for them and for their wives and children at
an immense price. Demetrius then laid before the
king the outlines of his method. A copy of the
original *Law of Moses* was to be obtained from
Eleazar, the high priest at Jerusalem. Six learned
men from each of the twelve tribes, competent for
the work of translation, were to be sent by him.
Aristeas and Andreas, who were the chosen depu-
ties, carried with them gifts and sacrifices of great
value, were received with great respect, and returned with all that was desired. The Jewish
elders were first tested by questions by Ptolemy
himself, and then shut up in separate cells in the
Island of Pharos. They agreed in the version

which each made, Demetrius writing it down. The work occupied seventy-two days, was approved by the king, and handsomely rewarded. This is the story, but it is evidently a fabrication. There were not seventy-two learned Greek scholars to be found in Palestine at that time, and certainly not six of each tribe. The numbers themselves betray the hand of the inventor. Demetrius, again, would not resort to such a method; and he was not alive at the time referred to. Moreover, the miraculous features of the narrative show that it was the product of a later age, and of the Rabbinical School. The *tradition*, however, such as it is, was handed down. It was repeated by Aristobulus in 125 B.C. It was added to by Philo, and believed by all the early fathers of the Christian Church; appearing in the writings of Irenæus, Clemens Alexandrinus, Eusebius, Athanasius, Cyril, Epiphanius, Jerome, Augustine, Chrysostom, Hilary of Poitiers, and Theodoret. *Jerome*, however, threw discredit upon it, and after his time it was received with considerable reserve. It is well to bear in mind that there was another tradition, which came from the Samaritans. *They* said that Ptolemy Philadelphus, hearing of the differences between the Jews and the Samaritans in respect to the Jewish law, called together a small body of translators, three of whom

were Samaritans, one was a Jew, and one assessor.
The Samaritans undertook to translate the Pentateuch, and the Jews the rest of the Scriptures. The
king approved of the version made by the Samaritans. This is no doubt a mere invention arising
out of the jealous feeling of the Samaritans, and
possibly from the fact that there were Samaritans
at Alexandria at that time. On the whole, the
probability is that the version originated quite
naturally from the requirements of the Jews in
Alexandria, as they adopted the Greek language,
and became less familiar with Hebrew and Chaldee. The Palestinian Jews were never favourable
to the Greek version. Hence it is likely that, in
process of time, an attempt would be made by
Hellenistic Jews in Egypt and elsewhere to *give
authority* to their Bible, and the fictitious letter of
Aristeas was written for that purpose. That the
letter *is* a fiction is evident from many internal
marks. It is written in the name of a Greek, but
is manifestly the composition of a Jew; and it
appeared at a time when such spurious productions
were common.

It is an interesting question how far the Septuagint has been founded on *earlier Greek versions.*
There is no impossibility in the case. Portions of
the Pentateuch may have been translated for the

use of Greek-speaking Jews *before* 285 B.C. That
the *earlier* books were rendered by a different
hand from the *later* is manifest in the Greek
itself. Traces of Egyptian influence, it is said,
can be discovered in the Pentateuch. There are
also forms and phrases of the Greek of Macedonia,
which, of course, would be used in Alexandria at
that time. The practice of reading and explaining
the Law in the Synagogues would very early lead
to the rendering of the Hebrew into Greek. And
when the books of the prophets were read, as they
were subsequently, the same necessity would lead
to *their* being translated. There were, we know,
other Greek versions, made at a much later date,
which the great Greek father, Origen, compared
with the Septuagint in his celebrated Hexapla.
But it is a remarkable fact that, however early the
Old Testament was translated into Greek, and
though the evidence is satisfactory that a portion
at least, probably the first six books, were placed
in the Alexandrian Library in the time of Ptolemy
Philadelphus, still *it was read almost exclusively
by the Jews.* "None of the Greek authors," says
Prideaux, "now extant, nor any of the ancient
Latins, have ever taken the least notice of it. For
all of them, in what they write of the Jews, give
accounts of them so vastly wide of what is con-

tained in the Holy Scriptures, as sufficiently show
that they never perused them, or knew anything
of them. There are, indeed, out of Eupolemus,
Abydenus, and other ancient writers now lost,
some fragments still preserved in Josephus, Eusebius, and other authors, which speak of the Jews
more agreeably to the Scripture history, but still
with such variations and such mixtures of falsity
that none of them remain, excepting only what we
find taken out of Demetrius, in the ninth book of
Eusebius, De Preparatione Evangelica, to give us
any ground to believe that the writers of these
ever consulted those books, or knew anything of
them. This Demetrius was a historian that wrote
in Greek, and an inhabitant of Alexandria, when
he compiled a history of the Jews, and continued
it down to the reign of the fourth Ptolemy, who
was Ptolemy Philopator, the grandson of Philadelphus. How much longer after this it was that
he lived is not anywhere said. He having written
so agreeably to the Scripture, this seems to prove
him to have been a Jew. However, if he were
otherwise, that is, not a Jew but a heathen Greek,
that no heathen writer but he only should make
use of those Scriptures, after they had been translated into Greek, sufficiently shows how much that
copy of them which was laid up in the King's

Library at Alexandria was then neglected, and also how carefully the Jews, who were the first composers of this version, kept and confined all other copies of it to their own use. "They had the stated lessons read out of it in their synagogues, and they had copies of it at home for their private use, and thus they seem to have reserved it wholly to themselves till our Saviour's time" (vol. ii. pp. 46, 47). Dr. Prideaux states the case perhaps too strongly. The fact that we have no traces of the use of the Septuagint among Greek writers is scarcely sufficient proof that the contents of the Mosaic law were unknown. Ewald makes a very different remark. "*As soon,*" he says, "*as these Greek versions began to circulate, they naturally became known by degrees, even without special effort, to the heathen philosophers, poets, and scholars of the day. In this way the first tolerably trustworthy medium was supplied them for making a closer acquaintance with Israel, and it could not fail to be instructive if we could trace in detail the impression produced on the heathen by those strange books, especially in the period when they first appeared*" (vol. v. p. 255). But although there may be differences of opinion as to the amount of influence which the Jewish Scriptures exercised over the minds of heathen writers, there

can be none at all as to the very rapid change
which took place in the Jewish mind, and which
continued for more than a century, by the close
connection of the Jews and Samaritans with the
heathen world.   It was about the time of the pro-
mulgation of the Greek version of the Scriptures
that *the Hellenistic School* of Jews arose, and it
will be necessary to give some account of its
characteristics and influence.

For a considerable period after the return of the
Jews from Babylon there still remained among
them a reluctance to draw closer the bonds of
fellowship with Gentile nations.   *The Babylonian
School* of Jews was quite as strict in all Jewish
doctrine and rites as that of Jerusalem.   But
events did much to break down that severity.   The
Persian wars, followed by those of Alexander, not
only scattered the people in various directions, but
led to many occasions of profitable intercourse with
the wealthy conquerors.   The Jews were oppressed
still, and multitudes of them were carried away
into slavery.   As they gradually obtained their
liberty it became necessary for them to seek out
means of livelihood, and they were thus brought
into closer contact with alien races.   This was
especially the case with those Jews who were either
transported by violence to Egypt or settled there

as emigrants. They very soon found opportunities of amassing wealth, and were tempted to lay aside the prejudices of their nation for the sake of pleasant and profitable friendship with their heathen neighbours. The children of the first generation of emigrants and emancipated slaves were in a very different position from their fathers. They were taught Greek as their native language, and were soon versed in the scholarship of Egypt. We cannot, therefore, be surprised that Greek philosophy and culture opened their stores freely to the more learned and intellectual Jews, and that they became cosmopolitan in their spirit. It was not a philosophy of antiquity which they were invited to study, but the systems which were in vogue in their own time, the representatives of which were in Alexandria exercising a powerful fascination over their contemporaries. It is true that there were different schools, which in some sense opposed one another. But they were all comparatively new to the Jewish mind, and perhaps as the Jews came from a system where variety of individual opinion was forbidden, and almost impossible, they would yield themselves all the more readily to the spell of Greek speculation.

The three great systems which had most attraction for the Jews were the Platonic, the Peri-

patetic, and the Stoic.   All had points of congruity
with the Old Testament.   The depth and idealism
of the old *Platonic* philosophy must have laid hold
with great force of the more profound spirits
among them ; and the *Stoic* severity and purity of
life matched well with the Jewish *ritual.*   There
were very few Jews who openly adhered to the
Epicurean system.   But it is well to remember
that while the learned Jews would *study* these
Greek philosophies, there was no occasion for them
to *renounce Judaism* in order to utilise their
newly-acquired wisdom.   They would naturally
turn to their own Scriptures, and try to find in
them all that the new teachers revealed to them.
This some of them did, to their own entire satisfaction, proving, as they thought, that Pythagoras
and Plato and Aristotle and Zeno had borrowed all
that was distinctive in their systems from the
Books of Moses.

It is a remarkable fact that at the very time
when the Jews were drinking deep at the fountains
of heathen thought and wisdom, they were de-
nouncing heathenism itself as a fanatical system, as
loudly as ever.   We can see this exemplified in the
later Books which were included in the Apocrypha,
in some of the strange fictions by which heathenish
practices were ridiculed, and in the Books, such as

Ecclesiasticus (written not very long after the Alexandrian connection began), the intention of which was to exalt the God of Israel and His people as against the ungodly of the Gentile world. "Like our scattered colonists in distant lands, the Grecian Jews would cling with double affection to the customs of their home, and invest with the halo of tender memories the sacred traditions of their faith. The Grecian Jew might well look with contempt, not unmingled with pity, on the idolatrous rites practised around, from which long ago the pitiless irony of Isaiah had torn the veil of beauty, to show the hideousness and unreality beneath. The dissoluteness of public and private life, the frivolity and aimlessness of their pursuits, political aspirations, popular assemblies, amusements—in short, the utter decay of society in all its phases would lie open to his gaze" (Edersheim). But notwithstanding this separation from heathenism, there was a recognition of a revelation of Divine truth in the midst of the darkness which led the better minds to make advances towards Greek philosophy. Some of the Rabbis denounced it, but it was studied notwithstanding. And the result was a new school among the Jews, a school of *Hellenising Jews*, who remained for centuries separate from the Jews of Palestine, and who introduced into what was subsequently their Bible the broader views of their *Hellenistic Judaism*. The Books which supported such views, and were included in the Septuagint, were at first somewhat countenanced by the Rabbinical party, but in the end they were denounced and forbidden, because they were supposed to exercise a kind of rationalistic influence over their readers, an influence which undermined the authority of the stricter Judaism. The contact between the Jewish and Greek minds, however, having been once brought about, could not be again resolved. The fact remained, that Jews read Greek literature, and were largely influenced by it. The school of Alexandria was too powerful to be ignored. The result was a compromise, as generally is the case, between *the written Word* and the *new tendency*. This compromise betrayed itself in some striking features of method, which we must briefly describe.

It has already been observed that the Jews of Alexandria preserved their traditional respect for the sanctity of the Jewish Temple at Jerusalem. The high priest of the nation was still regarded as a kind of ecclesiastical chief of the whole scattered Israel. The Old Testament was still the Authorised Scripture, which was not to be tampered with. But the study of Greek philosophy introduced into the minds of learned men in Egypt new thoughts, which they found it difficult to harmonise with the language of the Jewish Scriptures. This was especially the case in the speculations which the Platonists encouraged on the Divine essence. The Books of the Old Testament were written by men who believed in the personality of God, and who freely employed anthropomorphic representations in speaking of Divine intercourse with the patriarchs and prophets. In like manner had the Greek poets filled their writings with mythical and humanistic language, and creations of the imaginative genius which the philosophical minds of Greece had turned into mysteries and dim shadows of higher truths, discovering in them, or professing to discover in them, allegories which were full of the precious truth of a higher wisdom. Why might not the Books of the Old Testament, while still accepted as of Divine authority, be utilised, in a similar manner, by the new school of philosophical Jews? This, as we shall see, became a fixed principle of interpretation among those who remained faithful to the authority of Scripture, while surrendering themselves to Greek speculation. From the middle of the second century B.C. to the time of the Alexandrian School of the Christian Church, represented by Clemens Alexandrinus and Origen, the allegorical method prevailed. It was the source of great defection from the simplicity of faith, though at the same time it rendered some service to the cause of the true Church in attaching to it the more speculative minds, which would probably have held aloof otherwise from what could not be brought into any intelligible relation to their cherished philosophies. Ewald has remarked that there were prescriptions in the Book of the Law no longer applicable in their literal meaning, or of which the grounds were obscure, which by means of this allegorical method of interpretation still retained their sanctity, such as the regulations as to food and sacrifice. The history of the people, too, became a fruitful source of suggestion to such minds, from the account of creation downwards. There is scarcely any part of the Pentateuch which is not treated in this speculative manner by Philo, and he is said to have borrowed his ideas from previous writers; indeed, there are some traces of the same spirit in the Septuagint version itself.

But apart altogether from the connection which we have thus indicated between the Greek version and the Alexandrian School, there is a special interest to the Christian mind in the fact that the writings of the Old Testament were put into the hands of the Gentiles, and spread through a large extent of the world before the time of our Saviour. Although it was only a small portion of the Hebrew Bible which was placed at first in the Library of Alexandria, still it was the foundation on which the whole edifice of Greek Scriptures was subsequently reared. The remarks of Dr. Stanley, while somewhat too free, will be read with interest in connection with the facts which we have described: "If ever there was a translation which, by its importance, rose to a level with the original, it was this. It was not the original Hebrew, but the Septuagint translation through which the religious truths of Judaism became known to the Greek and the Roman. It was the Septuagint which was the Bible of the Evangelists and Apostles in the first century, and of the Christian Church for the first age of its existence, which is still the only recognised authorised text of the Eastern Church, and the basis of the only authorised text of the Latin Church. Widely as it differs from the Hebrew Scriptures, in form, in substance, in chronology, in language; unequal, imperfect, grotesque as are its renderings, it has, nevertheless, through large periods of ecclesiastical history, rivalled, if not superseded, those Scriptures them-

selves" (" History of the Jewish Church," v. 258-
9). To the critic the Greek version is of incalcul-
able value in preserving the traditional remembrance of the Hebrew where we have reason to
doubt the accuracy of our present Masoretic text.
And we may add that the additional Books which
were included in the Septuagint, and which we now
separate from the Old Testament, as the Jews of
Palestine did always, assist us to discriminate what
was given under inspiration of God from those
later writings, which, while they were read and
revered by the Alexandrian Jews, betrayed the
spiritual degeneracy of the nation, and the influence
both of heathen speculation and of Gentile manners.
The Apocrypha, as we shall be able to show hereafter, bears witness for God. It stands side by
side with the true Bible, but it seems to say to all
who read it, the holy men of God who wrote the
Books of the Old Testament spake as they were
moved by the Holy Ghost. A corrupt Bible is the
index as well as the fruit of a corrupt Church.

CHAPTER V.

THE APOCRYPHA.

THERE are many reasons why a close and accurate study of the collection of writings usually called the Apocrypha, is of special importance at the present time. We are in the midst of a controversy on the subject of Scripture authority. It is well that we should become familiarised with the grounds upon which the canonical books were separated from others, and it is, above all, necessary that we should estimate, more clearly and decisively than many do, the position of the Jews in Palestine, as distinguished from those in Alexandria. Some, who have given too little attention to the facts, are contented to admire passages here and there which they find in the Apocrypha, without regarding the sources from which such passages have come. They are apt to forget that the best words which are to be found in these later writings of the Jews were only echoes from the Old Testament. The light which

F

in some books shines upon the pages of the Apocrypha, and glows with Biblical, almost Christian,
splendour, is the *lingering light of the western sky.*
The contact of the Jewish mind with the Gentile
world produced, especially in the Alexandrian
writers, a considerable change in the style of
thought and language; in some cases, no doubt, a
broader tone and more philosophical spirit; but it
is certain that the Jews of the Hellenistic School,
from whom almost all the later didactic books
came, had no deep spiritual insight of their own,
and added nothing of permanent value to the body
of Divine truth already given to the world in the
canonical Scriptures.

Another reason why these books should be more
carefully studied is, that the fact may come more
prominently before us that there was a long interval of time between the closing of the Old
Testament and the production of these later books.
When we remember that there is nothing to be
ascribed to the period between Malachi and the
beginning of the second century B.C., at least with
any degree of certainty; that an interval must be
supposed of at least a hundred and fifty years,
during which the voice of the Jewish nation was
silent; and that such books as *Tobit, Baruch,* and
Ecclesiasticus, even if they should be dated at the

earliest period possible, still leave a broad space of time, marking off the canonical books from all others,—we must surely feel the force of the argument for the authority of the Old Testament.

And then we must add to these reasons another, which is perhaps still more striking ; these Apocryphal books come to us from the Alexandrian School, not from the Jews of Palestine. It is true that there is in them a great deal of strong Jewish feeling; they are defensive of Judaism; and in such books as Bel and the Dragon the writer plainly has the deliberate intention to exalt the religion of the Jews by sarcasm and ridicule against the heathen idolatry. Moreover, such writings as *The Wisdom of the Son of Sirach*, and *The Maccabees*, prove that there was no intentional departure from the old standpoint; no relaxing of Jewish nationality ; no desire to be absorbed in the Gentile world. The spirit of the Apocrypha, as a whole, is not really cosmopolitan, although it is here and there apologetic and conciliatory towards the best side of heathenism, especially in Ecclesiasticus and The Wisdom of Solomon. But the preservation of this lower class of Jewish literature did not, in the least degree, obscure the distinction, which remained clear and decided in the minds of the leading religious men of *Palestine*, however it was at Alexandria, between what was called the *first canon* and the *second canon.* The *"Deutero-canonical"* books were read, especially by the Hellenists and by the Jews who were of the Dispersion, but it is doubtful whether even the most advanced school of the philosophical Jews of Alexandria ever regarded the second canon, containing the Apocrypha, as possessing *Divine authority.* By the Jews of the Eastern schools they were quoted, and at first treated with respect; but at last they were condemned by the Rabbis, because their influence was thought to be unfavourable to the strict Judaism which resented the growth of Gentile influence: So that the result of this rise of a *second canon* was to confirm the authority of the *first.* It is true that in the early Christian·Church the familiar use of the Septuagint, into which, by degrees, the Apocrypha had been incorporated, led to the reading of the non-Scriptural books in the churches. But that may be accounted for from the fact that there was no disposition at that time to examine closely the authority of the books, and as they were included in the Greek Bible they would be often read as though they were inspired. And their general agreement with the Old Testament would be more thought of than their legendary and superstitious features, which would be less offensive in those early times than they are now. *But there never was a time when the books of the Apocrypha were not recognised as outside the line of canonical authority.* They were never quoted by any Apostolic writer. They never received the sanction of our Lord. As soon as the early Church entered upon the question of distinguishing Scripture from other books they were decisively relegated to a lower place.

There are many Jewish writings besides those which were included in the Septuagint. Without assuming to be able to give a perfectly exhaustive catalogue, we may mention the following as a tolerably complete enumeration of the works which were produced after the time of Malachi : Ecclesiasticus, Baruch, The Epistle of Jeremy, Tobit, The Wisdom of Solomon, Judith, I. Esdras, II. Esdras, Esther x.–xvi., the Song of the Three Holy Children, the History of Susannah, Bel and the Dragon, the Prayer of Manasses, I. Book of Maccabees, II. Book of Maccabees. All these are included in the Apocrypha. Then we are informed in the Talmud of other books which are not now extant, such as "*The Roll of the Building of the Temple*" and "*The Outside Books*," which are thought to have represented the works of heretics, as well as those of Hellenistic Jews, not recognised by the Rabbis. "In

the second, and even in the third century B.C.,
there were Hellenist historians, such as Eupolemus,
Artapanus, Demetrius, and Aristeas; tragic and
epic poets, such as Ezekiel, Pseudo-Philo, and
Theodotus, who, after the manner of the ancient
classical writers, but for their own purposes, described certain periods of Jewish history, or sang
of such themes as the Exodus, Jerusalem, or the
rape of Dinah" (Edersheim). These writers are
referred to by Eusebius, and extracts from them
are found in his Preparatio Evangelica (ix. 20, &c.).
But there are other works which have come down
to us which represent a distinct class of writings,
generally named the *Pseudepigraphic* or *Pseudo-
nymic*, because they were written with false names
of authors attached to them.   Dr. Edersheim, who
gives a very interesting account of these writings,
says : " It is difficult to arrange them otherwise
than chronologically, and even here the greatest
difference of opinion prevails. Their general character (with one exception) may be described as
anti-heathen, perhaps missionary, but chiefly as
Apocalyptic.   They were attempts at taking up
the keynote struck in the prophecies of Daniel;
rather, we should say, to lift the veil only partially
raised by him, and to point—alike as concerned
Israel and the kingdoms of the world—to the past,

the present, and the future, in the light of the kingship of the Messiah. Many of these works must have perished. In one of the latest of them (4 Esdras xiv. 44, 46) they are put down at seventy, probably a round number, having reference to the supposed number of the nations of the earth, or to every possible mode of interpreting Scripture. They are described as intended for the "wise among the people," probably those whom St. Paul, in the Christian sense, designates as "knowing the time" of the Advent of the Messiah. Viewed in this light, they embody the ardent aspirations and the inmost hopes of those who longed for the "consolation of Israel," as they understood it. The most interesting, as well as the oldest of these books, are those known as *"The Book of Enoch, The Sybilline Oracles, The Psalter of Solomon,* and *The Book of Jubilees, or Little Genesis"* (Edersheim). Then we have, in addition, *The Fourth Book of Esdras* (included in 2 Esdras, chapters iii.–xiv.), *The Ascension and Vision of Isaiah, The Assumption of Moses, The Apocalypse of Baruch, The Third Book of Maccabees,* found in the Greek Bible, probably dating about 50 B.C. ; *The Fourth Book of Maccabees,* included in the works of Josephus, but wrongly ascribed to him, probably 4 B.C.—an amplification of 2 Macc. vi. 18; vii. 42; *The Fifth Book of Maccabees*, written perhaps after the destruction of Jerusalem, containing the history of the Asmoneans and of Herod. (See Cotton's Maccabees, 1832; Stanley's Jewish Church, vol. iii.)

Now with regard to the books which we now call *The Apocrypha*, it must be remembered that they were placed side by side with the books of Scripture in the Septuagint by men who had fallen away from the strict notions of the Jews of Palestine. " Their ecclesiastical constitution was less definite, and the same influences which created among them an independent literature, disinclined them to regard with marked veneration more than the Law itself. The idea of a canon was foreign to their habits; and the fact that they possessed the sacred books, not merely in a translation, but in a translation made at several times, without any unity of plan or without any uniformity of execution, necessarily weakened that traditional feeling of their real connection which existed in Palestine" (Westcott, in Smith's Dict., art. Canon). At the same time it is evident that while the books were regarded as almost on a level with the Hagiographa, there was a distinction, even in Alexandria, between all such writings and those which preceded the Persian period. It does not follow because they were collected into the same volume with the Scriptures that they were esteemed as highly; for among the Alexandrians all literature on sacred subjects would be regarded with reverence.

There is very great variety in the books of the Apocrypha, and they cover a period of nearly two hundred years. The earliest cannot be dated before the third century B.C., and the latest was probably about 30 B.C., or later. Some portions were written by Christians after the time of our Lord. It was at the time of the Jewish revival under the Maccabees that the best of the extra Scriptural writings were gathered together, and when once such a collection was made it would be natural to add one and another until the political disturbances of Palestine and Egypt under the Roman power put an end to literary pursuits for a time. We must now proceed to characterise these Apocryphal books, — regarding them in their general features, and giving a short account of some which are the most valuable as revealing the religious state of the Jews.

1. The first and most conspicuous feature of these later books of the Jews is their *legendary and superstitious character*. This, it has been observed, may have arisen as a natural development of the national genius during the Captivity. The literary

and poetical gifts of the people would be called
out among the Babylonians and Persians.   In
1 Esdras iii. 4, there is an allusion to such gifts
and to the honours with which they were rewarded.
"The transition from this to the practice of story-
telling was, with the Jews, as afterwards with the
Arabs, easy and natural enough.   The period of
the captivity, with its strange adventures, and the
remoteness of the scenes connected with it, offered
a wide and attractive field to the imagination of
such narrators.   Sometimes, as in Bel and the
Dragon, the motive of such stories would be the
love of the marvellous mingling itself with the
feeling of scorn with which the Jew looked on the
idolater.   In other cases, as in Tobit, and Susannah
and the Elders, the story would gain popularity
from its ethical tendencies.   The singular variations in the text of the former book, indicate at
once the extent of its circulation and the liberties
taken by successive editors.   In the narrative of
Judith, again, there is probably something more
than the interest attaching to the history of the
past.   There is, indeed, too little evidence of the
truth of the narrative for us to look on it as history
at all, and it takes its place in the region of historical romance, written with a political motive.
Under the guise of the old Assyrian enemies of

Israel, the writer is covertly attacking the Syrian invaders against whom his countrymen were contending, stirring them up by a story of imagined or traditional heroism, to follow the example of Judith, as she had followed that of Jael. The development of this form of literature is, of course, compatible with a high degree of excellence, but it is true of it at all times, and was especially true of the literature of the ancient world, that it belongs rather to its later and feebler period. It is a special sign of decay in honesty and discernment when such writings are passed off and accepted as belonging to actual history" (Westcott in Smith's Dict., art. Apocrypha). At the same time it is well to notice that the legends of the Apocrypha are few and moderate in character compared with those of the Talmudical writings. In them there are not only fabulous stories with which are connected religious, moral, or political lessons and aims, but there are also legendary incidents introduced into the references to the Old Testament, especially in the era of Moses, whose life is embellished with wonders in the later times of the Jews, as we see in Josephus and Philo, and in some of the allusions in the New Testament. We should also connect with this fictitious element in the Apocrypha the spurious use of great names, as Ezra, Daniel, Esther, Jeremiah, Solomon. This would certainly not be attempted at a time when the greatest men were living, and when the Jewish Church was pervaded with the feeling of reverence for Scripture; it was the sign of a degenerate Church and a degenerate people.

2. Another characteristic of the Apocryphal writings is *the lower religious tone,* which expresses itself in ritualism, the advocacy of good works as the ground of acceptance before God, and the bigotry of national pride. The ritualistic extravagance is seen in such an instance as the description of Simon in the fiftieth chapter of Ecclesiasticus; but it may be observed that the rhetorical splendour of the words is perhaps almost more the aim of the writer than the exaltation of ritual itself. In many passages which it is unnecessary to quote, *good works* are dwelt upon as specially acceptable to God (see Tobit iv. 7–11, xii. 9); indeed it was the praise of almsgiving and the sanction of the worship of saints which no doubt led the Romish Church to cling to the Apocrypha, and include it in the canon by the decree of the Council of Trent. *National pride* was the leading element in the historical books, and in the mockery poured upon heathen nations. Even the best portions of such works as Ecclesiasticus and

the Wisdom of Solomon, are tainted with that in-
flated Judaism which was the sign of a falling
people. The mere rhetorical hero-worship which
we find in the Apocrypha is a very different thing
from the pious celebration of Divine goodness to
the fathers, which mingles with humble acknowledgment of unworthiness in the Psalms. The
record of great bravery and patriotism under the
Maccabees is rather like the outburst of feeling in
a people remembering a great past, and regretting
it, than the token of a vigorous spiritual life. It
was the despairing courage of a small band of
patriots rousing the nation for a while to great
efforts, rather than the calm strength of a great
people filled with the Spirit of God. There is
nothing throughout the Apocrypha which bears
witness to anything like a diffused and sustained religious life. The prophets were long gone, and the
prophetic spirit had not returned. The sages had
taken their place, and instead of Divine messages
were wise sayings and lofty flights of eloquence, and
attempts to clothe the predictions of the ancient
times with the new dress of sensational realism.
All was in vain. Rabbinism with its traditionalism,
Pharisaism with its worship of the letter of the law,
swallowed up every other form of religion except
in a few chosen spirits in the nation. The stricter

Jewish life became narrowed into a hateful bigotry
and intolerance and exclusiveness. The broader
Judaism which associated itself with the philosophy
of the Gentile world, and with the wider thoughts of
those who were seeking after God amid the varied life
of other nations, while it by no means restored the lost
tone of the prophets, certainly prepared the way, in
some degree, for a new revelation of Divine truth.

3. Much the most interesting feature in the
Apocrypha, however, is the presence there of what
may be called *a new religious philosophy*, which was
due to the influence of the Alexandrian school of
thought on the Jewish writers. This we must
briefly illustrate in a few examples, although the
fact is patent on the very surface of several of the
books. It has been observed by Dean Stanley that
the two writings which tower above all the rest,
have both a distinct object in view, and that connected with " wisdom," as the end sought after
by both Jews and Gentiles. The "*Wisdom of
the Son of Sirach*," the "*Wisdom of Solomon*," are
manifestly books of a similar character, connecting
links between the Old Testament and the New.
The Son of Sirach aims to enlighten the wise
men of Alexandria by a recommendation of Jewish
theology. The writer of the Wisdom of Solomon
aims to reconcile the Jewish mind to the specula-

tions of the Greeks. There is no doubt that the
Jewish book, the "*Wisdom of Joshua, or Jesus,*" is
earlier in date than the Alexandrian "*Wisdom of
Solomon.*" It is called *Ecclesiasticus,* because it
was the first of the "*Libri Ecclesiastici,*" that is,
books which were read in the Christian Churches,
though not canonical. "It was for the Jews of
Alexandria first, and therefore the Christians,
'*The Church Book,*' 'the favourite book of ecclesiastical edification,' 'the Whole Duty of Man,'
'the Imitation,' 'the summary of all virtues,' as it
was called in its original title" (The Jewish Church,
III., 267). We may place it at about the year 180
B.C. "The grandson of its author arrived in Alexandria in the close of the troubled reign of Ptolemy
Physcon (132 B.C.), the second of those kings who
were renowned amongst the Gentiles for bearing,
seriously or ironically, the name of 'benefactor'
(Euergetes). When amongst his countrymen in
the foreign land, he discovered 'no slight difference of education,' and at the same time a keen
desire to become instructed in the customs of their
fathers, he found no task more worthy of his labour,
knowledge, and sleepless study than to translate
into Greek this collection of all that was most practical in the precepts and most inspiring in the
history of his people. Jerusalem is still the centre

and Palestine the horizon of his thoughts. A priesthood, with their offerings, their dues, and their stately appearance, are to him the most prominent figures of the Jewish community. Nor is the modern institution of the scribes forgotten. He draws his images of grandeur from the cedars of Lebanon, and the fir-trees that clothe the sides of Hermon, from the terebinth with its spreading branches; his images of beauty from the palm-trees in the tropical heat of Engedi, or from the roses, and lilies, and fragrant shade by the well-watered gardens of Jericho. The drops of bitterness which well up amidst his exuberant flow of patriotic thanksgiving are all discharged within that narrow range of vision, which fixed his whole theological and national animosity on the three hostile tribes that penned in the little Jewish colony,—the Edomites on the south, the Philistines on the west, and the Samaritans on the north. And in accordance with this local and almost provincial limitation is the absence of those wider oriental or western aspects which abound in other canonical or Deutero-canonical books of this period. It is, after Malachi, the one specimen of a purely Palestinian treatise during this period" (Stanley, III., 268).

This book was written in Hebrew, and translated into Greek by the grandson of the author. The

short preface, which is attached by the translator
or by some other hand, evidently aims to connect
the book with the earlier writings of the prophets.
The Joshua who wrote the book had a grandfather
Joshua, who " lived after the people had been led
away captive and called home again, and almost
after all the prophets." He was " a man of great
diligence and wisdom among the Hebrews, who did
not only gather the grave and short sentences of
wise men that had been before him, but himself
also uttered some of his own, full of much understanding and wisdom." The book was begun by
the elder Joshua, left unfinished to his son Sirach,
and handed on to the Joshua or Jesus, the son of
Sirach, who gave it his name, compiling it into one
volume, " intituling it both by his own name, his
father's name, and his grandfather's." The grandson of the writer of the book tells us that he has
translated it into Greek, and asks pardon " wherein
we may seem to come short of some words, which
we have laboured to interpret. For the same
things uttered in Hebrew and translated into
another tongue have not the same force in them;
and not only these things, but *the law itself and
the prophets and the rest of the books*, have no
small difference when they are spoken in their own
language." He sets it forth " for them also, which

G

in a strange country are willing to learn, *being prepared before in manners to live after the law*." There is rather a mixture in the book of the old and the new. In some places the moral law is placed above the ceremonial, but in others the ceremonial is exalted. There is a tone of mild wisdom running through the whole, which plainly is intended to attract the foreigner and harmonise with the broader spirit of the Gentile world ; at the same time there is a strong national feeling expressed at times, and especially at the end, in the celebration of the heroes of old, " Let us now praise famous men and the fathers that begat us." The hero-worship which begins in remote antiquity culminates in the magnificent description of the typical *Simon the Just*, who probably lived about the time of the grandfather of the author. The book was well adapted for its purpose, to recommend Jewish thought and custom to the Alexandrians.

But the other work which we have mentioned, *The Wisdom of Solomon*, though its object was similar, to conciliate the Greek mind and the Jewish to one another, is very different and probably much later in date. Some, as Jerome and others of the Fathers, have ascribed it to Philo ; though it is not likely to have been composed so

late as his time. Some have even traced, as they
supposed, the hand of a Christian. It is best
regarded as proceeding from the Alexandrian
school of devout, contemplative Judaism, and
was possibly written about a hundred years before Christ. The whole subject of its authorship
and date is still under discussion, and cannot as
yet be decided. But the character of the book
forbids the supposition that it was written by a
Christian hand. As coming from Alexandria it is a
most impressive and deeply interesting illustration
of the influence of philosophical thought on the
Jewish mind. We must reserve a full examination
of its doctrine as preparatory to Christianity to a
later opportunity. Meanwhile we would draw attention to the very distinct mixture of philosophy
with religion which, although, as the title seems
to imply, there may be some early indications in
the writings of Solomon of a tendency which
might be developed into some such form, was
yet a new feature in Jewish thought, and almost
unknown in Palestine in such bold utterances.
There can be no doubt that the writer of the
" Wisdom of Solomon" was a Platonist. Such
lofty teaching was suited to the atmosphere of
Alexandria, and was taken up by men like Philo,
" who laboured to show that all that was true and

good in heathen speculations could be found in
the Law of Moses and in the writings of the
prophets." " *The spirit of the Lord filleth the
world, and that which containeth all things hath
knowledge of the voice.*" " *Wisdom, which is the
worker of all things, taught me ; for in her is an
understanding spirit, holy, one only, manifold,
subtle, lively, clear, undefiled, plain, not subject to
hurt, loving the thing that is good, quick, which
cannot be letted, ready to do good, etc. She passeth
and goeth through all things by reason of her
pureness. For she is the breath of the power of
God, and a pure influence flowing from the glory
of the Almighty ; therefore can no defiled thing fall
into her. For she is the brightness of the Everlasting Light, the unspotted mirror of the power of
God, and the image of His goodness. And being
but one she can do all things ; and remaining in
herself she maketh all things new, and in all ages,
entering into holy souls, she maketh them friends of
God and prophets*" (Wisdom vii. 22–27). "*Pre-
ludings of a high philosophy and faith,*" these may
be said to be, as Dean Stanley calls them. They
were more than philosophical ; they were deeply
religious. They express the yearning of the Alexandrian mind after the higher revelations, which
were supplied by the more definite teaching of

Christianity. *Immortality* and *Resurrection* are very clearly there—though not as in the Gospel of Christ, *based upon facts.* The preciousness of the soul is connected with the Divine Truth and Love. *" God created man to be immortal, and made him an image of His own eternity. To know God is perfect righteousness. To know His power is the root of immortality "* (Wisdom iii. 2, iv. 13, v. 15, xv. 3). But it must not be forgotten that this book stands, in some sense, by itself in the Apocrypha. Even the Wisdom of the Son of Sirach does not approach it in elevation of language. The other books of these later centuries, while they give us the evidence of great tenacity of national feeling among the Jews, betray a laxness of religious life, a general feebleness and self-righteousness, which show that the Books of Wisdom were the composition of *sages*, who were no proper examples of the people generally; while in some of the later compositions, as Esdras and Esther, there is a wild excitement of Messianic expectation, betokening the spirit of despondency and of fanaticism which had taken the place of vital religion.

CHAPTER VI.

THE SCRIBES AND THEIR TRADITIONS.

THERE is no more important fact in the history of the Jewish people than the change which was necessitated in their mode of worship, and in their religion generally, by the *national disintegration* which took place in the two captivities, of the ten tribes to Assyria, and of Judah to Babylon. There could be nothing like the old Temple worship resumed in the land of their oppressors. The generation which grew up in Mesopotamia must have depended upon *congregational services* for their mutual instruction and edification, in so far as it was public and united. It is not likely, however, that in the "strange land" *edifices* would be erected, especially as the captivity would endure but seventy years, and the people would be continually reminded by their prophets and preachers that the Temple would be rebuilt and the worship of former times restored. The "*congregation*" was recognised from the beginning of the nation. And it would seem that the Greek word "*synagogue*" was at first employed as exactly equivalent to the Hebrew words which represented the *gathering together of the people in an appointed meeting and to one place.* The word "*House*" was added when the custom of meeting in one building became fixed.

It is remarkable that the Jews themselves have held that synagogues are very ancient, even dating from patriarchal times. In the time of the prophets there certainly must have been "gatherings," which resembled the subsequent services held in . synagogues. In 2 Kings iv. 23 there is an allusion to such periodical meetings. The prophets were preachers, and they were disconnected altogether from the Temple. The existing books of prophecy are the remains of ministries, in some cases extending over many years, exercised, it is true, in various places, but by means chiefly of popular gatherings. We can well imagine, therefore, that when the Temple was destroyed the religious life of the Jews was maintained by congregational worship. The Book of Ezekiel contains several very pointed allusions to such gatherings, and the ministries of Ezra and Nehemiah must have given a fresh impetus to what was virtually an institution, the regular service of an assembly. At what time synagogues were erected it is impossible to say, but we cannot be far wrong if we assign them to the period of Ezra, when the Scriptures were re-published and no doubt began to be copied and spread once more among the people. Maimonides tells us that the rule became fixed, that where there were "ten persons of full age and free condition always at leisure to attend a religious service, there a synagogue was to be erected." Ten such persons were considered the nucleus of a permanent congregation or church, that the services might be punctually performed.

Now the service of the synagogue consisted mainly in the reading of the Scriptures and the offering of prayers. At first there is no doubt that the reading was confined to the Pentateuch; but in later times, and probably from the closing of the Old Testament Canon, about the third century before Christ, the reading of the prophets was added to that of the Law, and eventually the Hagiographa was admitted into the service. It will be seen at once that this systematising of the public gatherings and solemn reading of the Scriptures amongst the people, would enlarge the number of those who devoted themselves to the work of multiplying copies of the sacred books, and of reading them intelligently to the congregation.

Out of such a beginning there came great issues. The whole religious life of the Jews was most materially affected by the rise of the school of *Scribes*, which might be said to follow upon the period of prophetic ministry, and which developed the very powerful element of *Rabbinism*, dominant for centuries in the synagogues of the East, both in Palestine and in Mesopotamia; and at the time of our Lord the prevailing religious influence among the educated and strict Jews, especially at Jerusalem. We must describe briefly the growth of this remarkable element in the Jewish religious world, for without a clear understanding of the state of mind which characterised the Jews of Palestine and the East generally, we cannot appreciate the importance of that division which took place about three centuries before Christ in the religious views of the people. Those who came under the influence of Gentile thought in Egypt formed a school of Judaism very different from the school of the Scribes. *Traditionalism* may be said to be the main feature of the Eastern Jews who remained in Palestine. While separate from that traditionalism, really although not nominally opposed to it, there grew up in Egypt the school of philosophical Jews, who made less of traditions because they made more of the broader and more human teaching of the Old Testament. How it was that *traditions* came to be so vital a part of the religion of the Scribes we must now explain.

The fundamental fact round which the whole of the Jewish religion gathered, was the giving of the Law to Moses upon Mount Sinai. Upon that Law as a basis the constitution in Church and State was built up. The Books of Moses, which contained the records of that special Divine revelation at Sinai, were the Pentateuch, which the Jews called *The Law* or *Thorah*, because of the close connection of all contained in those books with the worship of the Temple and the constitution of the nation. But after the giving of the Law there were other Divine gifts, as the wisdom of the elders, the expositions and interpretations which first were orally delivered by Moses himself to his contemporaries, and then subsequently were embodied in the writings of the prophets and psalmists, and others who were under the power of Inspiration. This, in distinction from the written Thorah, was *the Kabbala*, that which was "*received*" from God. At first, and probably until about two centuries before Christ, the view held in regard to this inspiration outside the Thorah was that it was authoritative but secondary. Hence the Prophets and Hagiographa were never placed in exactly the same position as the Pentateuch, and until the time of Simon the Just, about three hundred years before Christ, were not publicly read in the syna-, gogue. But there grew up, in course of time, an immense amount of traditional matter, some of which no doubt was very ancient and of genuine worth, as having come down through Ezra from the best days of the Jewish Church; but other traditions were the result of the studies and public expositions of the Scribes.

When a passage out of the Law was read from the ancient Scriptures, which were written in Hebrew, it was necessary to expound the meaning of it, besides translating the very words themselves, in the current language of the people, which was Chaldee or Aramaic, varying with the district where the synagogue was situated. The interpreting scribe was the *Meturgeman*, and the interpretation itself was the *Targum*. These Targums were for a time, no doubt, mere extempore discourses, but they were remembered and at last . were written down. Hence we find, shortly before the time of our Lord, the celebrated Targum of Onkelos, and about two hundred years afterwards the Targum of Jonathan.

But the preservation of the Targums was by no means all that came out of the school of the

Scribes and the study of the Scriptures after the
Captivity. There was another result which was
perhaps even more momentous in its influence on
the Jewish people. The motto which Simon the
Just is said to have left behind him was prophetic.
It pointed to the developments of the Rabbinical
school. "Be careful in judgment, set up many
Talmidim (*i.e.*, learned men), and make a hedge
about the Thorah." The prosperity of the Jewish
world, he said, depended "on faithfulness to the
Law of Moses, on preservation of the Levitical
worship, and on works of righteousness." This is
the true basis of the religion which grew up after
Simon's time during the three centuries which
preceded Christianity. Learned Rabbis did arise,
and they were multiplied. They studied the Law,
and in order to make a hedge of defence about it,
they taught the doctrine that the authority of
traditions was equal to, if not greater than that of
the written Law. The writing down of those
traditions was not at first necessary, because they
were comparatively few and might be remembered,
but they naturally had to be written as they multiplied and were mingled with the comments and
opinions of successive teachers. The current view
was that Ezra and his contemporaries collected the
chief traditions and handed them down; but they

(the Rabbis) can give no authority for this beyond the mention of a line of learned men, as, *e.g.*, Antigonus of Socho, Joses Ben Jochanan, Joses Ben Joezer, Nathan the Arbelite, Joshua Ben Perachiah, Judah Ben Tabbai and Simeon Ben Shabach, Shemaiah and Abtalion, Hillel and Shammai, and so on to Simeon, Gamaliel, Simeon Ben Gamaliel and Gamaliel Ben Simeon, and others, to Rabbi Judah Hakkadosh, who is said to have written them down in the Mishna. There were traditions of all kinds, corrections of the text, various readings, explanations, paraphrases, ritual expansions, rubrics, and then opinions and illustrations, fables and myths, which became an almost immeasurable accumulation of the learning and folly of scholars and preachers during five hundred years, and perhaps for a still longer time.

The Talmud is formed of three parts, which are supposed to include the bulk of this tradition. *The Mishna*, or Second Law, is the original text of the traditions, and the two *Gemaras*, one emanating from Jerusalem and the other from Babylon, contain learned commentaries upon the Mishna, the one of the fourth and the other of the sixth century of our era. There was another important distinction which the Jews held in regard to these writings. Some of them were *Halacha*,

i.e., doctrines and rules of life—those which concerned the walk of the faithful Jew ("*Halach*"
meaning to walk), others were *Haggadha* (that
which is said), expositions and illustrations, which
were of a broader and looser character, like the
pleadings of an advocate in distinction from the
decisions of a judge. The Mishna contains both
Halacha and Haggadha, *i.e.*, both rules and commentary, and was itself an accumulation of sixty-
three tractates, divided into chapters and verses;
and then followed the miscellaneous mass of traditions and opinions which is found in the later
books of the Gemaras. "In course of time," says
Dr. Edersheim (whose account of the Talmud is very
full and interesting in his "Life and Times of
Jesus the Messiah," vol. i., chapter viii.), "the discussions, illustrations, explanations, and additions
to which the Mishna gave rise, whether in its
application or in the Academies of the Rabbis, were
authoritatively collected and edited in what are
known as the two *Talmuds* or *Gemaras*. If we
imagine something combining law reports, a Rabbinical 'Hansard,' and notes of a theological debat-
ing club—all thoroughly Oriental, full of digres-
sions, anecdotes, quaint sayings, fancies, legends,
and too often of what, from its profanity, superstitions, and even obscenity, could scarcely be

quoted, we may form some general idea of what the Talmud is."

But there is one kind of tradition which we must admit is of the greatest value in the transmission of the sacred writings. That is the *Masora*, a tradition of the Jewish scribes themselves in copying the Scriptures. The copyists were accustomed to write down on the margins of their copies, and wherever they could find space, not only traditional readings varying from the text, but many different kinds of notes, which were held to be worth preserving, with respect to the Scripture. These traditions remained for centuries locked up in manuscripts, and hidden from the public eye by a strange enigmatical method of writing; but they were partly deciphered and published in the sixteenth century by a great Jewish scholar who became a Christian, Rabbi Jacob Ben Chayim. He was followed by another great scholar, Elias Levita, who published the "Massoreth Hammasoreth," (Traditio Traditionis), 1538. These works prepared the way, though at an interval of three hundred and fifty years, for the edition of the Masora lately published by Dr. Ginsburg, who has devoted a quarter of a century to his laborious inquiries, and has collected the traditional readings and comments of centuries into one great

work.   The result of this toil cannot be estimated.
Our present Hebrew Bible is received by us without question at the hands of the later Jews of the
sixth century.   We are now able to compare it
with the traditions which have come down through
many ages, and which, when placed side by side
with all the different forms of the text which can
be gathered from the Targums and from the Talmud, as well as from ancient versions, will enable
us to purge away any errors which have crept into
the Authorised Text, and so to obtain, as nearly
as possible, the very words of the sacred writers.
Had the Rabbis devoted themselves in the same
manner to the preservation of the exact form of
the sacred books which they have to the accumulation of their opinions and usages, the Old Testament would have been handed down to us in a
more perfect state, and the toil of our modern
scholar would have been rendered unnecessary.

But what was Rabbinism, regarded as an element
in the religious life of the Jewish people?   We
must clearly understand the difference between the
spirit of these traditions, whether we regard them
in the Targums, or in the Talmud, or in the Masora,
and the spirit of the Old Testament.   This distinction has a most important bearing on the general
subject with which we are concerned in these

chapters, viz., the preparation which was made in the Jewish people for the new doctrine, the "Truth as it was in Christ Jesus." Now the evidence of the Targums is very valuable as showing that the farther we go back the more authority seems to have been attached to the written Word of God, the less to the mere explanations and illustrations which were added. The *later* Targums, as those of Jonathan Ben Uzziel, and that of Jerusalem, were full of extraneous matter which corrupted the Word of God; but the following account of the earliest Targum, that of Onkelos, given by the late Emanuel Deutsch, in Smith's Dictionary of the Bible, will show that the earlier Scribes had no intention to overlay the Bible with tradition. "The language of the Targum is Chaldee, closely approaching in purity of idiom to that of Ezra and Daniel. It follows a sober and clear, though not a slavish, exegesis, and keeps as closely and minutely to the text as is at all consistent with its purpose, viz., to be chiefly and above all, a version for the people. Its explanations of difficult and obscure passages bear ample witness to the competence of those who gave it its final shape, and infused into it a rare unity. It is always concise and clear and dignified, worthy of the grandeur of its subject. It avoids the legendary character with which all

H

the later Targums entwine the Biblical word, as
far as even circumstances allow. Only in the
poetical passages it was compelled to yield, though
reluctantly, to the popular craving for Haggadah;
but even here it chooses and selects with rare taste
and tact. Generally and broadly it may be stated
that alterations are never attempted, save for the
sake of clearness; tropical terms are dissolved by
judicious circumlocutions, for the correctness of
which the authors and editors—in possession of
the living tradition of a language still written, if
not spoken in their day—certainly seem better
judges than some modern critics, who, through
their own incomplete acquaintance with the idiom,
injudiciously blame Onkelos. Highly characteristic
is the aversion of the Targum to anthropopathies
and anthropomorphisms; in fact, to any term which
could in the eyes of the multitudes lower the idea
of the Highest Being. Yet there are many passages retained in which human affections and
qualities are attributed to Him. He speaks, He
sees, He hears, He smells the odour of sacrifice, is
angry, repents, &c. The Targum thus showing
itself entirely opposed to the allegorising and
symbolising tendencies which in those, and still
more in later days, were prone to transform
Biblical history itself into the most extraordinary

legends and fairy tales, with or without a moral.
The Targum, however, while retaining terms like
the arm of God, the right hand of God, the finger
of God,—for power, Providence, &c., replaces terms
like foot, front, back of God, by the fitting figura-
tive meaning. We must notice, further, its repug-
nance to bring the Divine Being into too close
contact, as it were, with man. It erects a kind of
reverential barrier, a sort of invisible medium of
awful reverence, between the Creator and the creature. Thus, terms like 'the Word' (Logos, Sansc.
Oîn), the Shechinah (Holy Presence of God's majesty, 'the Glory'); further, human beings talk-
ing not *to* but *before* God, are frequent. The same
care, in a minor degree, is taken of the dignity of
the person of the patriarchs, who, though the Scripture may expose their weaknesses, were not to be
held up in their iniquities before the multitude,
whose ancestors and ideals they were. That the
most curious ὕστερα πρότερα and anachronisms
occur, such as Jacob studying the Thorah in the
academy of Shem, &c., is due to the then current
typifying tendencies of the Haggadah. Some extremely cautious, withal poetical, alterations also
occur when the patriarchs speak of having acquired
something by violent means; as Jacob (Gen. xlviii.
22) by his 'sword and bow,' which two words be-

come in the Targum, 'prayers and supplications;' but the points of the Targum which deserve serious study are those which treat of prayer, study of the Law, prophecy, angelology, and the Messiah."

It will be seen from this description of the most ancient Targum, that while the full-blown Rabbinism of the Talmud is not to be found there, the germ of much which was afterwards developed can be recognised. The absence of direct spiritual manifestations in prophets who were able to testify to what God had spoken to them, led to a superstitious use of the Scripture, and an endeavour to supply the deficiency of personal inspiration by means of a doctrine of *"emanations," Sephiroth,* of which there were said to be ten, viz., Crown, Wisdom, Intelligence, Mercy, Judgment, Beauty, Triumph, Praise, Foundation, Kingdom. The basis of this doctrine was the necessity for some medium of intercourse between the infinite and the finite. The first of these emanations, " *The Crown,*" was the source of all the others, " *En-Soph,*" the Fountain of Light. This may be a dim perception of the truth which, no doubt, underlies all the teaching of the Old Testament, that God comes into the world that He may bring back the world to Himself; but the real principle which was at work in the minds of the later Jews was the dread of anthropomorphism, the worship of the Divine majesty, the sense of estrangement from God, and therefore the fear of offending Him by undue familiarity. We recognise the same loss of fellowship in the distinction which the Rabbis made so emphatic between the justice of God and the mercy of God. They were groping in the dark. They had renounced the great truth of the Divine Fatherhood. They were going about to establish a righteousness of their own which should satisfy the claims of Divine justice, and they had ceased to believe in the Divine righteousness as the gift of Divine love.

It is very interesting to notice the attempt to qualify the idea of Divine revelation by such terms as *Memra* and *Shechinah*, which no doubt arose from the felt necessity of some veil upon the countenance of God, lest man should be consumed by its brightness. The term *Memra* occurs 179 times in the Targum Onkelos, and very many times in other Targums. The word seems to point to some kind of *medium of revelation*. It is thought by some learned writers to be distinguishable from the Logos. And the term *Shechinah* is employed along with it, though as distinct from it. There seems to be the idea of personification included in both, and yet they are not used as identical with "*Messiah.*" Rather the words would appear to be a

recollection of the whole system of revelation
which was vouchsafed to the fathers, and which
included both personal appearances and glorious
manifestations. , To some degree such language
may be said to represent the lingering light on the
horizon, the remains of primitive revelation; but
it also bears witness to the darkness which was
deepening in the minds of the Jewish people.
They were satisfying themselves with such terms
instead of the simple and practical phraseology of
the Scriptures. We see the results in the growth
of philosophical mysticism in such men as Philo of
Alexandria, and in the rapid deterioration of the
Rabbinical schools which soon substituted the
follies of the Scribes for the doctrine of the Inspired
Word. The Rabbis set the traditions of their
schools above the written Bible. "He who busies
himself with Scripture only, has merit and yet no
merit." They professed the greatest reverence for
the letter of Scripture, but, like the Roman Catho-
lics, they regarded it as a mystery which was committed to those who were learned in the traditions
to unfold. The "hedge about the Law" was of
greater importance than the Law itself, so that, as
the Lord Jesus told them, they "made void the
Law through their traditions." The Sanhedrim is
declared to be "the foundation-stone of the oral

law and the pillars of the doctrine; and from them the statute and the judgment goes forth to all Israel. They have the warrant of the law, for it is said, 'According to the sentence of the Law which they shall teach thee,' &c. (Deut. xvii. 11), which is an affirmative precept, and every one who believes in Moses our master, and in his Law, is bound to rest the practice of the Law on them, and to lean on them" (Hilchoth Mamrim, c. i. 1). And yet, strangely enough, the infallibility of the Sanhedrim is denied by the Rabbis. They were not bound to follow any particular council, but only that which is largest and wisest. It has been well said, by an anonymous writer on the subject, that " the defectiveness, inconsistency, and falsehood manifested in the testimony of the Rabbis on the authority of the Sanhedrim is sufficient to throw discredit on all their claims. They have not only no proof from Scripture, but are not able themselves to find in tradition an unbroken chain of testimony. They fail at the very outset. After producing two links they leave a chasm of above two hundred years unaccounted for."

Rabbinism was a usurpation of the learned class, seeking by means of a false authority to obtain power over the mass of the nation. The old hierarchy had, in fact, perished, and the power of

the Pontificate had passed away. Rabbinism sought
to succeed to that power. There was no distinct
body of doctrine which could be identified with
the Rabbis. "They had no system of theology,
only what ideas, conjectures, or fancies the Haggadah yielded, concerning God, angels, demons,
man, his future destiny and present position,
and Israel with its past history and future glory.
What a terrible mass of conflicting statements and
debasing superstitions; legendary colouring of
Biblical narratives and scenes, incongruous and
degrading to them ; the Almighty Himself and His
angels taking part in the conversations of Rabbis
and the discussions of Academies ; nay, forming a
kind of heavenly Sanhedrim, which occasionally
require the aid of an earthly Rabbi! The miraculous merges into the ridiculous, and even the
revolting. Miraculous cures, miraculous supplies,
miraculous help, all for the glory of the great
Rabbis, who by a look or word can kill and restore
to life. At their bidding the eyes of a rival fall
out and are again inserted. Nay, such was the
veneration due to Rabbis, that Rabbi Joshua used
to kiss the stone on which Rabbi Eliezer sat and
lectured, saying : 'This stone is like Mount Sinai,
and he who sat on it like the ark !' Modern
ingenuity has, indeed, striven to suggest deeper

symbolical meaning for such stories. But it may
be asserted, without fear of well-grounded contra-
diction, that if, in respect of substance, there is not
a difference, but a total divergence of fundamental
principles between Rabbinism and the New Testament, comparison between them is not possible as
regards their spirit.   Here then is absolute con-
trariety" (Edersheim).   And to these remarks it
may be added that the spirit of Rabbinical traditionalism was just as truly a departure from the
teaching of the Old Testament as it was reproved
and contradicted by the New.   There are very
few quotations in the Talmud from the books of
the Old Testament.   Most of those in the Mishna
are taken from the Pentateuch.   "References to
any other Old Testament books are generally
loosely made, and serve chiefly as *points d'appui*
for Rabbinical sayings.   Scriptural quotations
occur in 51 out of the 63 tractates of the Mishna,
the number of verses quoted being 430."   The
chief object of the Talmud is to glorify the Rabbis,
not to open the meaning of God's Book.   This, no
doubt, was partly the result of the legal spirit
which prevailed among the Scribes.   They began
with the worship of the Law simply as Law.   The
worship of Law must necessarily produce a *legalism*
in the spirit of the people.   " It lies in the nature

of every such law, of every informal, half-systematic code, that it raises questions which it does not solve. Circumstances change, while the Law remains the same. The infinite variety of life presents cases which it has not contemplated. A Roman or a Greek jurist would have dealt with them on general principles of equity or polity. The Jewish teacher could recognise no principles beyond the precepts of the Law. To him they all stood on the same footing, were all equally Divine. All possible cases must be brought within their range, decided by their authority. The result showed that in this, as in other instances, the idolatry of the letter was destructive of the very reverence in which it had originated. Step by step the Scribes were led to conclusions at which we may believe the earlier representatives of the order would have started back with horror. Decisions on fresh questions were accumulated into a complex system of casuistry. The new precepts, still transmitted orally, more precisely fitting into the circumstances of men's lives than the old, came practically to take its place. 'The words of the Scribes' were honoured above the Law. It was a greater crime to offend against them than against the Law. They were as wine, while the precepts of the Law were as water" (Dr. E. H. Plumptre, art. Scribes, Smith's Dict.).

But there was one result of this degeneracy of the learned class among the Jews which has been overruled, in the providence of God, to the welfare of His people and the promotion of His glory. The wide separation which took place between the writings of such men and of those who were under their influence, and the sacred books which they continued nominally to hold in reverence, greatly assisted subsequent ages in the determination of the authority of Scripture. We can plainly distinguish between the inspiration which was embodied in the Old Testament and the usurped authority of mere ecclesiastics and scholars. Whether we look into the Talmud or into the Apocrypha it is evident that the Spirit of God had ceased to speak as of old. There are utterances here and there in both which remind us that the truth of God still exercised a powerful influence over the hearts of men; but such utterances are rather like reflections of what had been already given to the world in a previous age, than fresh and original vouchsafements. And it is remarkable that the most valuable of these reflections of the Old Testament teaching are not to be found among the Rabbis of Palestine or Mesopotamia, but in the region where the light of the Old Testament was beginning to mingle with that which had been discernible among the most cultured of the heathen, which had gleamed, if it could not be said that it had shone like a sun in the heavens, in Greek sages and Alexandrian scholars. · Thus the facts of history became prophetic. The Word of God was about to be taken from those who would not follow its guidance, and would be given to another nation, to the whole world, that the fruits thereof might be brought forth; that the ancient promise might be fulfilled, that in the covenant made with Abraham "all the families of the earth should be blessed." The Scribe who is instructed to that larger kingdom is not one that is learned in Rabbinical lore, but one that has sat at the feet of Him "of whom Moses in the Law, and the Prophets, did write, Jesus of Nazareth," "the Son of God, the King of Israel."

CHAPTER VII.

THE RISE OF JEWISH SECTS.

THE history of the Jewish Church is full of very striking lessons. None, perhaps, is more significant than that which we learn from a close attention to the facts connected with the development of *Jewish Sects*. It is remarkable that, amidst all changes and disturbances in the Jewish mind, from the time of the Restoration from Captivity onwards, there was nothing that could be properly described as the appearance of a *sect*, until about two centuries before the Christian era. One might have expected that the vigorous work of reformation carried on by Ezra and his successor, Nehemiah, and others of the Great Synagogue, would not merely have awakened a spirit of opposition, which it undoubtedly did, in those who were more or less under the influence of Gentile thought and life, but have led to the initiation of distinct *religious parties*, with separate designations, within the limits of the Jewish Church. But there is no

evidence that there was any such *formal* resistance
to the Judaistic revival. If it had existed in any
other shape than a laxness of religious life on the
part of individuals, it would certainly have revealed
itself in some form which would be regarded as
part of history. But, while it has been attempted,
by some scholars of the German school, to prove
that the influence of such a party is to be traced
in books of the Old Testament, as, *e.g.*, in Jonah,
the argument breaks down. It is fatal to such a
view that *there is no literature outside the Scriptures which can be assigned to the period immediately following upon Nehemiah and Malachi*, which
there certainly would have been had the reforms
carried out by Ezra produced anything like a theological division among the people.

The rise of the *Egyptian School* of Judaism is
a fact quite distinct, and enables us, by its distinct-
ness, to study the more accurately the development
of Judaism in Palestine. It was a natural result
of the favour shown to Jews by the Ptolemies, and
the rapid growth of Greek influence, through the
power which the Seleucidæ had in Palestine, all of
which we may date from about 285 B.C. to 185 B.C.,
that is about a hundred years—that vast numbers
of Jewish people, both within and without the Holy
Land itself, renounced the extreme strictness of

former times; and, while preserving their external
allegiance to Jerusalem, were more and more withdrawn from it in spirit and life. But it must be
remembered that in the great majority of instances
this widening of thought and relaxation of discipline was accompanied by a *moral corruption*,
and often by an imitation of heathen *manners*,
which threatened the entire destruction of the
nation. There were great abuses, no doubt, at
Jerusalem itself, in the rule of the High Priests.
But so long as the temple service was maintained
there was a rallying point for Judaism. And we
may believe that the synagogue worship, which
had increased largely after the time of Ezra, and
was spread over Palestine, supported, as it was,
by the reading of the Scriptures, as the fathers had
delivered them, especially of the Pentateuch, contributed to keep alive, in many hearts, the hope
that a Divine blessing would yet be poured out on
Jerusalem. It was the work of Divine Providence,
however, in the external events of the world,
which brought about the climax from which we
must date the revival of Judaism.

Now it would be a great misapprehension of the
facts to suppose, as some have done, that there was,
for two hundred years, a *large-minded and catholic-
spirited school* among the Jews, who desired to

find all that was true and healthy among the heathen religions and modes of life and thought, in order to amalgamate it with a progressive Judaism. *There is no evidence of any such school.* There were individuals who, by their contact with Greek philosophy, about two hundred and fifty years B.C., were led to think that they might fulfil the hopes of their people for universal dominion by influencing the leading minds of other nations to study the religious views of the Jewish nation, and to become proselytes. But there was no *school* of rationalistic or catholic Jews *out of Egypt. The Jews of Palestine must be regarded as the true Jewish Church.* In that, until the end of the third century before Christ, there was no appearance of division, though there was no doubt much indifference and moral corruption. The real cause of a new state of things was the disturbance of the political atmosphere.

For fifty years and more the two great neighbouring powers of Syria and Egypt, represented by the Seleucidæ and the Ptolemies, made the intermediate country of Palestine a battle-ground for supremacy. The effect was very disastrous on the Jewish people. Not only were they exposed to the evils of war, but their leading men were seduced into a most demoralising connection with

the rival powers, leading them to disgraceful acts
of treachery to their own nation. It was still
more injurious to the interests of the Jewish
religion that the Greek power, which ruled from
the centre of Antioch, at last gained the victory
over the degenerate family of the Ptolemies. *Antioch* could exercise a much more direct and irre-
sistible influence than *Egypt*. Alexandria was, no
doubt, the most learned city, but learning does
not always go with political supremacy. The
Greek mind was dominant. Although it was
speedily to succumb before the rising military
power of Rome, still for a time it prevailed in the
lingering remnants of Alexander's empire. The
tyranny and corruption of the Syrian rulers came,
as a blast of trouble, to quicken into flame the
dying embers of religious and patriotic zeal in
the hearts of the Jewish people. From 203 B.C.
to 198 B.C., it must have been evident to all true-
minded Jews that unless there was a rising-up of
their national life against their oppressors, they
would be crushed into absolute ruin, between the
upper and nether millstones. " The decisive contest which was impending was in the most inexorable manner driving all the still hidden impulses
of the age, both good and evil, into the light of
day, so as to bring out clearly what was within the

I

power of those who represented the aim and the force of the whole period of the new Jerusalem, viz., the pious" (Ewald).

It will not be possible in this place to describe the course of events which led to the revival of Judaism. The extraordinary family of the Asmoneans or Maccabees were, no doubt, only representatives of a large number of zealots, who were brought out of their obscurity by the force of great events. Mattathias, the father of Judas Maccabæus, was a man himself of 'great character, and the ruling spirit of his time. He must not, however, be regarded as an adventurer, called out by political troubles. He was a religious devotee, inspired to great efforts by the danger which threatened the future of his people, regarded as the people of Jehovah, and dependent upon the temple at Jerusalem. It was "*the abomination of desolation*" witnessed in the holy place which roused the Maccabees and their companions to fury. It was the recovery of the temple and the revival of the religious position of Judaism, which, identified as it was with their political prosperity, became the ruling aim of the patriots. And the rise of sects in the Jewish Church dates from this remarkable period. The Sadducees, Pharisees, Essenes, and others had no distinct existence before the Maccabean Revival. They took their character from the religious elements at work at that time.

In several places in the Books of the Maccabees we find a reference to what is there called "*the Mingling.*" By this is intended *the "mingling" of Jews with Gentiles,* beyond the permission of the Law of Moses. From the time of Ezra, who protested so strongly and practically against the laxness of the people in their intercourse with surrounding nations, there had, no doubt, been a party among the Jews of Palestine which was, more or less, opposed to strict Judaism. But it is an error to suppose that this party was recognised as representing any *religious authority.* It was simply *the moral refuse* of the nation. There was a school of sages, but they must be distinguished from the political men who, for their own selfish ends, played into the hands of Gentile rulers. But it is not wonderful that there should be a conviction still surviving in Palestine, that the old Ezra-spirit was the true safety of the nation. On the basis of the Law of Moses the Jewish State rested. Those who really loved Israel would be faithful to the Law. Hence arose, during the Greek period, a band of *religious patriots,* who were called the *Chasidim* by the Jews, and *the Assideans* by the Greeks. They were *the godly* or *pious,* the *Puritans* of that

time, who resisted the process which, they felt, was
fatal both to religious and to national prosperity,
of intimacy with, and imitation of, the heathen.
Now it has been alleged by some that, long before
the time of the Maccabean Reformation there was
a school of broad thinkers and heretics who derived
their origin from one Antigonus of Socho, through
a disciple Zadok, and flourished in the first half of
the third century B.C.   But the tradition, if it can
be said to be worthy of the name, is quite worthless.   It is now generally agreed that *the Sadducees*
could not have received their name from. *Zadok*,
nor have come into existence as early as the third
century.   There are historians of the rationalistic
school, like Ewald, who would fain persuade us
that the Sadducees were a continuation of a school
of thinkers among the Jews, who had been in
existence from the time of Ezra, but their view is
not borne out by evidence.   *The Chasídím were
the true beginning of both the Pharisees and
Sadducees.*

For a considerable time, at least fifty years, there
was only the one name and the one party, that of
the *religious zealots*, who were identified with the
Maccabees.   A few references to these are made in
the books which describe the history of the great
struggle with Antiochus Epiphanes and his suc-

cessors. There were freethinkers, no doubt, at that time; but Ewald himself admits (vol. v. p. 282), "They were not yet called *Sadducees*, but simply the '*lawless*' or ungodly, and sometimes, in stronger language, '*sinners.*'" This clearly proves that there was no practical recognition, at that time, of the necessity of intellectual orthodoxy. There was substantially no difference of creed among the Jews; but the school of the Pious or Chasîdîm was formed for the better observance of the Law as a rule of worship and life. "*They recovered the Law out of the hand of the Gentiles and out of the hand of kings, neither suffered they the sinner to triumph*" (1 Macc. ii. 48). It has been suggested by Dr. Edersheim ("Life and Times of Jesus the Messiah," vol. i. p. 323) that both the names of the two religious sects were given them with reference to the original designation of the "*godly.*" There would naturally arise two parties out of such a movement as that which was commenced by the Maccabees. Some would be prepared to go any length in the cause of reformation and faithfulness to the Law. Others would consider themselves the *moderate* party, and they would be likely to be the richer and more worldly men, who did not feel the obligations of religion so supreme, but sought to conciliate the heathen rulers. The zealots became *Pharisees*, that is, *"Perushim," the separated* ones, who would be regarded by themselves as the only pious, but in the eyes of their opponents were *" righteous over much."* Dr. Edersheim 'thinks that in contrast with this extreme party, those who would be regarded as the representatives of moderation were called *" The Righteous," i.e.,* those who laid more stress on *practical righteousness* than on punctilious observance of the letter of the Law, *" Zaddiquim"* or *Sadducees.* " There is, indeed, an admitted linguistic difficulty in the change of the sound *i* into *u* (Zaddiquim into Zadduquim), but may it not have been that this was accomplished, not grammatically, but by popular witticism ?   Such mode of giving a ' by-name ' to a party or government is, at least, not irrational, nor is it uncommon.   Some wit might have suggested—Read not *'Zaddiquim,'* the righteous, but *' Zadduquim '* (from Zadu), ' desolation,' ' destruction.' Whether or not this suggestion approves itself to critics, the derivation of Sadducees from Zaddiquim is certainly that which offers most probability." The question of *names* is, however, of comparatively little importance.   It is certain that both parties, both the Pharisees and Sadducees, were faithful to Judaism so far as external attachment was concerned.   They remained within the Synagogue. They were not "separatists" in the modern sense of the word; neither were they driven away from Judaism by any adverse decree of the council.

But there was a remarkable body of men who appear somewhere about that time, or a little later, the *Essenes* or *Essœi*, numbering at the most only about four thousand, who withdrew themselves from the Temple and from the worship of the Jews, and retired into a kind of hermit life, for the purpose of carrying out vows of celibacy and asceticism. But little is known of them. They are not mentioned in any book of the New Testament, and not very distinctly in the writings of the Rabbis. But they are referred to with great respect by Philo and Josephus. Whether they were, at the earliest time, what they afterwards became, it is impossible to say; but their name seems to denote that they were "*outsiders*," and their peculiar views would exclude them from fellowship with the orthodox Jews. In some respects they were connected with both Pharisees and Sadducees. They perhaps borrowed from the former their extreme views of purification, and from the latter their denial of the Resurrection. But while there would be points of sympathy, it seems most probable that the Essenes were simply Jews who

had been influenced by the Parsee religion, which,
at that time, began to affect powerfully the creed
of the more western nations. They worshipped the
sun and held the evil of matter, which were two of
the leading distinctions of the Persian religion.
They might be said to be in some sense the fore-
runners of the gnostics, who, three centuries later,
seriously affected the doctrine of the Christian
Church.

These remarkable *"outsiders"* were the only instance of a break in the external uniformity of the
Jewish Church, and as they numbered so few and
removed so entirely away from the neighbourhood
of Jerusalem, they can scarcely be said to form an
exception to the rule of adherence to the synagogue, which the Jews observed so consistently
through many ages. Their unique character sets
off very distinctly the true features of the Pharisees and the Sadducees, and shows that we should
greatly misapprehend the position of those two
parties in the Jewish Church if we regarded them
as in any sense contending for the supremacy of
rule, and attempting to exclude one another. They
represented rather tendencies of thought and life
than opposing sects. They corresponded more with
the different schools of theology which now exist
within the same Established Church in our own

country—such as the High Church and the Broad
Church—than with the distinct religious denomina-
tions of our time, worshipping with different rites
and in different sanctuaries. Pharisees and Sadducees alike recognised the Scriptures as their authority, and nominally, at least, united in maintaining
the services of the Jewish Temple. This is an important fact, because it shows us very clearly that the
extra-scriptural books did not proceed from either
of these so-called sects, unless they were such
books as the Maccabees, which had a merely historical authority; or, as in the case of the Second
Book of the Maccabees, were intended to exalt the
martyrs of Judaism. Such works as Ecclesiasticus,
and the Wisdom of Solomon, and Tobit, and
Judith, and the Book of Enoch, and the Psalter
of Solomon, and other such writings, although
those who wrote them might have been attached
to one or other party among the Jews, were certainly not put forth with any sectarian bias, or for
any purpose of rivalling the authority of Scripture.
In some cases their aim was merely to help the
Jews to be faithful to their Law; in others, to help
the Gentiles to study the Jewish Scriptures; and
in others, to promote the Messianic sentiment,
which, as time went on, became a source of consolation to those who were weary of their national

troubles. There is no evidence that the Jewish Church, as represented by its leading teachers and councils, ever placed such works side by side with their ancient Scriptures. They were called "*The outside books*," and as such were looked upon as identified with the "*outsiders*." We cannot, of course, at this distance of time, specify which books were so stamped with disapproval. Some, no doubt, for their piety would be favourably regarded. But it is certain that the extravagant doctrines which are found in later books, especially on the subject of angels, and the fabulous stories which mingled with historical records, as we see in the Second Book of Maccabees and others, were not formally sanctioned by the Jews as though they were in books of Scripture. There is a great difference between the miracles of Scripture and those in the extra-scriptural books, and between the theology of the prophets and that of the post-prophetic times. Thus the Word of God stands by itself. The Jews with all their faults did not wilfully tamper with their Scriptures. The different parties in their Church kept watch over one another, and Pharisees and Sadducees alike appealed to the same standard of faith.

In confirmation of this view we cannot bring forward a better witness than the rationalistic critic,

Ewald. Speaking of the Pharisees, he says that during the period of persecution and external trouble it was of little importance to find exact Scripture authority for their beliefs, because they were beliefs that were the demand of the age. "But piety had no sooner gained the upper hand in the nation than it began to confound with the instruments of its triumph the source from which it had obtained them; it placed the Holy Scriptures still higher, and paid them a more scrupulous veneration than ever before" (v. 365). "In respect of the substance of their teachings, they proceeded wholly in accord with the grand line of development which had been running through strict Judaism ever since the days of Ezra. They placed the Law above everything else, without on that account rejecting the other records, traditions, and usages of religion inherited from the past; they approved of the customary interpretation of Scripture, without commending the extravagance of allegory which was striving to prevail, and in other respects were glad to attach themselves somewhat closely in every way to national and established practices, as well as to good moral principles, such as reverence for age. Of Greek philosophy and foreign literature they did not seek much knowledge, nor did

their origin permit them to, though they were too
prudent to repudiate it altogether in this age. But
they well understood that their power over the
people depended particularly on the knowledge
and application of the Holy Scripture, and some of
their ablest teachers accordingly occupied themselves in establishing a special service of the Law
with the further view of being able to dispute with
the Sadducees on all important subjects" (p. 368).
Thus it is evident that the Pharisees were great
preservers and defenders of the Word of God. But
as we know that they were opposed by the Sadducees, and the Sadducees were, on some points,
such as the doctrine of angels and the future life,
certainly condemned by the teaching of the Old
Testament, as the Lord Jesus Christ distinctly told
them, we are naturally led to ask, whether the
existence of the less orthodox school, for a hundred
and fifty years before Christ, may be taken as any
argument against the view which we are accustomed to hold of the Jewish Scriptures, viz., that
they were received without a dissentient voice in
the Jewish Church as the supreme authority in
doctrine and life. We will, in concluding this brief
notice of the Jewish sects, give our remaining space
to this important point.

The one chief distinction between the Sadducees

and the Pharisees consisted in the denial, on the part of the former, of the authority attached by the latter to *the Oral Law.* We have already referred to this subject. The traditions of the scribes were no doubt very ancient. But it was not until the rise of the Pharisaic school that they were persistently ascribed to Moses himself. The attempt was made, on the part of the Traditionalists, to suppress by such means all opposition to the teaching of tradition. Now the Sadducees did not deny the value of traditions as such. But they distinctly opposed the attempt to manufacture an *external sanction* by the falsification of history. They revered the general authority of the fathers, but they distinguished between the Word of God and the customs which had accumulated in the course of ages. The result was that the authority of the Scriptures was confirmed. An appeal to *the written Word* at any time silenced discussion, as we see in the instance of our Lord's rebuke of the Sadducees. They did not dare to deny what was on the page of Scripture, though they had suffered a false view of its meaning to remain among them. The later Sadducees had no doubt carried much further than their predecessors the sceptical tendency which had arisen among them. At first they were simply *remonstrants* against an extreme traditionalism; but they soon became *doubters* on some of the doctrines of the orthodox creed. The Pentateuch, which alone was regarded as the *legal standard* of reference on disputed points of belief, contained no distinct statement of the doctrine of man's resurrection after death. But after the Captivity, whether under the influence of heathen teaching or as a natural effect from the many troubles which came upon the people, the doctrine of a future life and of a resurrection from the dead became a leading point of the orthodox creed. The Pharisees, who maintained it strongly, sought support for their view outside the letter of Scripture, in the traditions of the fathers—and, perhaps, were inclined to put the later Scriptures higher in authority, and almost on a level with the Pentateuch, for their argument's sake—such a doctrine, they said, *could* not have been left by God uncertain. If it was not on the face of the Law, it must have been communicated orally. "A supplementary tradition was necessary, indispensable. This tradition exists. Moses received the Law from Sinai, transmitted it to Joshua, Joshua to the Elders, the Elders transmitted it to the Prophets, and the Prophets to the men of the Great Synagogue" (Klein). Now the Sadducees in opposing this theory did real service to the cause of Scripture authority. Just as in the Reformation, Luther and his followers, by their opposition to the Roman Catholic view of tradition, brought out more clearly and positively the great principle of Protestantism, " the Bible and the Bible alone," so these opponents of traditionalism in. the Jewish Church, while not themselves sound in the faith, were witnesses for the Word of God. It may be a matter of surprise that the Sadducees should have rejected the existence of angels or spirits. But it is not certain that even those of our Lord's days denied a spiritual world. altogether, but only the traditional views which were current as to angelic ministry and the complicated system of angelic existences which we find in such "outside works " as the *Book of Enoch*. There is no trace, either in the writings of Josephus or of the Rabbis, of an entire denial of angelic existence on the part of the Sadducees. Possibly some of their number went farther than others, and sank into a lower depth of scepticism. But the main point to which we desire to draw attention, is the concurrence of both sects in upholding the authority of the Scriptures. The Pharisees assumed to be more reverent towards Scripture than their opponents, maintaining that the touch of the sacred book defiled the hands; but the Sadducees, in denying that doctrine of defilement, only resisted the extreme ceremonialism of the Pharisees. It must never be forgotten that they were both parties *within* the Jewish Church. There was no real *break up* of the religious system and unity. The Scriptures, as they came down to the time of Christianity, were the deposit which the Jews, with all their faults, faithfully kept and handed on to their successors. Notwithstanding the rise among them of divisions of opinion and practice, especially in the observances of the Law, there was no desire on the part of any portion of the Jewish nation to renounce the standard given them by Divine Inspiration. From the time of the Maccabees, at latest, the written Word was a clearly defined limit, and it was never wilfully transgressed.

CHAPTER VIII.

THE GROWTH OF THE MESSIANIC EXPECTATION.

IT is matter of history that, at the time when our Lord Jesus Christ came into the world, there was a widespread expectation of a personal Deliverer. The testimonies of Tacitus and Suetonius, the visit of the Magi to Bethlehem, and other well-known facts, point to the prevalence of such feeling among heathen nations. Some would account for this by the intercommunication between Jews and Gentiles, which had become common for many years before Christ. Whether this was so or not can scarcely be now determined. It is, however, an interesting question, which is not beyond the limits of research, though occasionally surrounded with obscurity ;—what was the growth of the Messianic expectation from the time when the Jews were no longer visited by inspired prophets ? We must not be perplexed by what appears, at first sight, an enigma, that, with the canon of Scripture in their hands, so little was really understood and

K

believed by the Jewish people concerning their promised Deliverer.

After the restoration of the religious and political commonwealth in the time of Ezra and Nehemiah, it was natural that the chief attention of the Scribes, and those who followed their guidance, should be directed to the observance and preservation of the Law. No doubt there was always included in the conception of the Law that of the kingdom of God. But as the spiritual life of the people declined, and as political troubles absorbed their attention, the true theocratic idea became buried in the heap of confusion, brought upon the nation by their difficult and dangerous position between Syria and Egypt. It must not be forgotten, as is well observed by Dr. Edersheim, that in the Old Testament "the Messiah and His history are not presented as something separated from, or superadded to, Israel. The history, the institutions, and the predictions of Israel ran up into Him." We look back from a personal narrative to the Old Testament, and find there predictions or anticipations on almost every page, which were fulfilled in Christ; but while the personal facts were still in the future, it required more insight than was common among the people to separate the substance from the shadow. At the same time it is evident, from the later writings of the Rabbis, that there was, all along the ages from the time of the prophets, a clear and decided *expectation*. Sometimes it was obscured by the more exciting thoughts which were stirred by events of the day; but it was never completely lost. The general and deeply laid confidence in a Divine vocation and in a future Divine restoration kept alive the more particular hope that a son of David would appear, who would be the ideal Israel, the Prince of God, the Prophet, Priest, and King. The Rabbis perverted the Scripture, and lowered the expectation to the level of their own unspiritual minds; but the evidence of their own writings, which they themselves declare to be a revival of the tradition of the elders, proves that the main ideas of the Old Testament were, at least, nominally preserved. Dr. Edersheim states that "a careful perusal of their Scripture quotations shows that the main postulates of the New Testament concerning the Messiah are fully supported by Rabbinic statements. Thus, such doctrines as the *premundane existence* of the Messiah, His *elevation* above Moses, and even above the angels, His *representative* character, His cruel *sufferings* and *derision*, His *violent death*, and that *for His people*, His *work* on behalf of the living and of the dead, His *redemption* and restoration of Israel, the *opposition* of the Gentiles, their partial *judgment* and *conversion*, the prevalence of His Law, the *universal blessings* of the latter days, and His *kingdom*, can be clearly deduced from unquestioned passages in ancient Rabbinic writings. Only, as we might expect, all is there indistinct, incoherent, unexplained, and from a much lower standpoint" (vol. i. pp. 364, 365).

As we might naturally conclude, the Septuagint, being under the influence of the Alexandrian school, seems to make light of the hope of Israel, or rather to sublimate it into philosophical terminology, which deprived it of the real and personal element which it retained in the old Hebrew language. In the passage of Isaiah (chap. ix. 6) which seems to predict the Divine Sonship of the Messiah, the Seventy have toned down the words into "*Angel of the great Council;*" though another reading is nearer the Hebrew. "Among the Jews of Egypt," says Dr. Payne Smith, "a belief in a personal Messiah soon entirely ceased. Thus, whereas in Psalm cx. 3, the words of the Hebrew are 'Of the womb of the morning is the dew of thy birth,' the Septuagint paraphrases it thus, 'Of the womb have I begotten thee before the morning dawn.' They acknowledge the pre-existence of the Messiah, but were offended at the doctrine of His birth in time. Their idea probably was a kind of Arianism, that the Messiah was a superior angel or pre-angelic being. But their chief dread was anthropomorphism, bringing God down to the level of man."

It has been sometimes remarked that there is no indication of Messianic expectation in the Apocrypha. But that is only partly correct. There is no distinct allusion to the personal Messiah by name, but in several books there is an undercurrent of hope which evidently rests upon the promises given to the fathers. The Book of *Ecclesiasticus* dates, according to some critics, from before the time of the Maccabees, and, as Ewald has observed, "The Messianic hopes are expressed in it with plenty of force in various passages," though the general tone of the work is rather expository and practical than predictive. The House of David is singled out as the line of rule, and the triumph of Israel in the future is clearly set forth (see Ecclus. iv. 15; x. 13–17; xi. 5, 59; xxxii. 17–19; xxxiii. 1–12; xxxvi. 11–17; xxxvii. 25; xxxix. 23; xlv. 25, 59; xlviii. 10, 15). Again, in *the first Book of Maccabees* we read, "*The Jews and priests were well pleased that Simon should be their governor and high priest for ever, until there should arise a faithful prophet*" (xiv. 41). They pulled down the stones of the defiled Temple and laid them up, we are told, "in the mountain of the Temple in a convenient place, *until there should come a prophet to show what should be done with them*" (iv. 46). "Thus," says Ewald, "in the slow course of the centuries the Messianic hope penetrates once more without resistance through all their feelings, not merely in periods of deep distress and longing, but in those also of the highest exaltation and joy; without this outlook and expectation there is no pure satisfaction and tranquillity. In the book called *The Wisdom of Solomon*, dating probably as late as 50 B.C., or even still nearer the Christian era, and coming from the philosophical school, we meet with the doctrine of the Logos, so prominently expressed that the work has been ascribed to Philo, whose writings are filled with that term, though employed in an Alexandrian sense. The character of the true Ruler, and the manner in which He is to become so, are exhibited at the close in language of the utmost eloquence and power. It is, indeed, only the Messianic hopes of eternal retribution and judgment which here take the deepest hold; and all the turns and steps of the discourse have their original type in the Old Testament" (Ewald). "*Thine almighty word leaped down from heaven out of Thy royal throne, as a fierce man of war into the midst of a land of destruction." "It touched the heavens, but it stood upon the earth." "In all things, O Lord, Thou didst magnify Thy people and glorify them, neither didst Thou lightly regard them, but didst assist them in every time and place"* (Wisd. xviii. 15, 16, 19, 22). The whole teaching of the book is the personification of Divine Wisdom and Love, which was evidently regarded as the doctrine of the Old Testament, and blended with the hope of a personal Deliverer. The Alexandrian School, however, were inclined to sink the expectation in a wider philosophico-religious system. Some of the books now included in the Apocrypha are of very late origin, as, *e.g.*, the Second Esdras (or fourth Book of Esdras, as it is sometimes called), which was probably written by a Christian about a hundred years after Christ. It is chiefly Apocalyptic in character, and is of no value as evidence of the Jewish expectations before Christ.

There are several remarkable remains of the period between the time of the Maccabees and the Christian era, which we must now notice. They leave us in no uncertainty as to the prevalence of Messianic expectations. Indeed, they clearly show that during the last hundred years of the pre-

Christian period, the predictions of Messiah were very prominently before the Jewish mind, and became something like a fever of anticipation. This was especially the case after the Roman conquest of Jerusalem under Pompey, when the political state of Palestine was one of great depression and fear. Then the people began to look for a Deliverer from heaven as they had never done before, and the worldly-minded amongst them found the language of Scripture suit their purpose as they put into it their own sordid and ambitious views.

The Books of the Sibylline Oracles (see Fridlieb, *Oracula Sibyllina*, 1852) is a very mingled collection of Greek verses in twelve books, with several fragments.   Most of the work is worthless, as it was the composition of Christians, endeavouring to support Christianity by forging predictions which correspond to the facts of Christian history.   There is one book, however, the third, which is regarded by critics as dating from the middle of the second century before Christ.   This part of the work was composed by a Hellenist Jew, and is full of allusion to the Messianic hope.   We find a picture drawn of the times of the Messiah in verses 652 to 807, and on this, it is generally admitted, *Virgil* founded the

predictions of the golden age which he has introduced in his fourth Eclogue, and which is found
also in *Hesiod* [Works and Days, 109], and in
Ovid in his Metamorphoses, Book I. 89 (cf.
Euseb., Præp. Evan., i. 7; xii. 13). Messiah is
described as *the King sent from heaven*, who
would judge every man in blood and splendour of
fire (vers. 285, 286). He is the *King whom God
will send from the sun.* Whether these Sibylline
verses are the genuine remains of heathen antiquity
or not must remain doubtful. Oracles of the
Sibyls are referred to by Plato, Aristotle, Varro,
Dionysius of Halicarnassus, and Livy; but if there
ever were such, they probably perished, and the
mere fact that they had existed was employed as
a basis on which to build up the forgeries of later
times.

But of much greater value than those oracles is
the remarkable book on which a great deal has
been written during the last half century, *The
Book of Enoch*—and from which it is supposed by
some that a quotation is made in the Epistle of
Jude (vers. 14, 15). Archbishop Laurence published a translation of an Ethiopic version in 1838,
but since that time other manuscripts have been
collected, and a new translation made by Professor
Dillmann (Leipzig, 1853). It is supposed to have

been originally written in Hebrew or Aramaic, but we possess no other remains of it than we find either in Ethiopic or Greek. Some have professed to be able to recognise three different elements in the work : (1.) *An original portion,* chapters i. to xxxvi., and lxxii. to cv., which is supposed to date about 175 B.C. (2.) *The Parables,* chapters xxxvii. to liv. 6; lv. 3 to lix.; lxi. to lxiv.; lxix. 26 to lxxi. This portion is dated about the time of Herod the Great. (3.) *The Noachian Sections,* together with chapters cvi., cvii., and the later conclusion in cviii., as to the date of all which chapters there is great doubt. It is impossible here to refer more directly to these chapters, but one or two quotations from what is now regarded as the oldest portion of the work will give an idea of its general character. *" He will go forth from His habitations, the Holy and Mighty One, the God of the world, who will hereafter tread upon Mount Sinai; appear with His hosts, and be manifested in the strength of His power from heaven. All shall be afraid, and the watchers shall be terrified."* *" Behold He comes with ten thousand of His saints, to execute judgment upon them, and destroy the wicked, and reprove all the carnal for everything which the sinful and ungodly have done and committed against Him "* (chaps. i., ii.) . This may be said to be the *text* on which the book is written. It is a description of the judgment which shall be executed on the ungodly, and an exhortation to the righteous to stand firm and be patient: *"In these days, saith the Lord, they shall call to the children of the earth, and make them listen to their wisdom. Show them that you are their leaders; and that renumeration shall take place over the whole earth; for I and my Son will for ever hold communion with them in the paths of uprightness, while they are still alive. Peace shall be yours. Rejoice, children of integrity, in the truth"* (chap. civ.) Dr. Edersheim thinks that Professor Schürer has conclusively shown that *The Parables* are pre-Christian in date, and they are full of Messianic allusions. In this portion of the work *"Messiah appears by the side of the Ancient of Days, His face like the appearance of a man, and yet so lovely, like that of one of the holy angels. This 'Son of Man' has, and with Him dwells, all righteousness; He reveals the treasures of all that is hidden, being chosen by the Lord, is superior to all and destined to subdue and destroy all the powers and kingdoms of wickedness* (chap. xlvi.) *Although only revealed at the last, His name had been named before God, before sun or stars were created. He is the staff on which the righteous lean, the light of nations, and the hope of all who mourn in spirit. All are to bow down before Him, and adore Him, and for this He was chosen, and hidden with God before the world was created, and will continue before Him for ever* (chap. xlviii.) *This ' Elect One' is to sit on the throne of glory and dwell among His saints; heaven and earth would be removed, and only the saints would abide on the renewed earth* (chap. xlv.) *He is mighty in all the secrets of righteousness, and un-righteousness would flee as a shadow, because His glory looked from eternity to eternity, and His power from generation to generation* (chap. xlix.) *Then would the Earth, Hades, and Hell give up their dead, and Messiah, sitting on His throne, would select and own the just, and open up all the secrets of wisdom, amidst the universal joy of ransomed earth"* (chaps. li., lxi., lxii.)

The remarks of Ewald on the Book of Enoch are so full of interest that it will be well to introduce them here at length. "The anxious inquiry into the course and issue of human history, and the zealous search for the finger of God in the great stages both of past and future, even in separate events, had been from the first in Israel a true pro-phetic task. But the attempt to adapt, with a certain nicety, the period of the past to an appar-

ently sacred and Divine member, in order to infer
from it with the more confidence a Divine termina-
tion of their sufferings and trials, only came into
fashion in those last centuries, in the complete
extinction of the living prophetic ministry. For
in this age the long and seemingly unproductive
lapse of time during which the Messianic expectation was awaiting its fulfilment had given to this
hope a greater tension and solicitude, while the
historical survey of all ages embraced a much wider
scope and was much better trained; and the prophetic writer, because he could be nothing more
than a writer, had now more leisure and induce-
ment for the learned pursuit of such historical contemplations. The longer the accomplishment of
the Messianic hope was delayed, the further did
the prophetic historical survey, impelled by a sort
of internal necessity, extend itself over the remotest
past, as though it could find no rest until it
reached the two extreme limits of universal history
itself. Some of the authors of the Book of Enoch,
accordingly, have striven to fathom the primeval
ages of Christianity. Amid these they have fixed
their gaze chiefly on the appearance and spiritual
significance of Enoch, distinguished in the most
wonderful way among the patriarchs of this earliest
epoch of the world. As the first pious man, stand-

ing at the highest stage of holiness, and living not
too long before the Flood, he seemed the fittest to
discourse with deep emphasis from his distant and
elevated point, covering the sins of the whole
world and their consequences, to describe in grand
pictures the steps of universal history pre-deter-
mined from eternity down to its anticipated end;
and to set forth the ultimate advent of the Messianic salvation as certain to arrive, even though late,
and not till after many and long vicissitudes.   At
the same time one writer specially avails himself
of the opportunity, as Enoch had once been known
as the protector of all deeper inquiry and knowledge, and had consequently been himself regarded
as the first great sage of the world, to make him
proclaim, as though it was the result of his own
experience, a sort of deeper view into the whole
structure of the universe and the realm of spirits.
This noble grasp of all the wonders of history and
of the spiritual and physical world, and the attempt to combine all these departments more
perfectly together, and employ them collectively
for exhortation, constitute the second novelty in
this book.   The great diffuseness which naturally
results, especially in comparison with the rapid
verity of the Book of Daniel, proves that in the
form in which we now have it the book is, as it

were, the precipitate of a literature, once very
active, which revolved in this age round Enoch.
Though, however, his exhortations flow on in a
broad stream, they are, at the same time, well
calculated to seize and terrify the mind ; and it is
these, together with the fragments and signs of
secret wisdom which it contains, that must have
procured for it a very large number of readers in
that day.   It succeeded in hitting off with sufficient power what there was to be said at the time ;
and its earliest portions, which appeared in fugi-
tive leaves, are directed with the utmost keenness
against the heathen potentates and their allies "
(v. pp. 347–349).

Another relic of the pre-Christian times is the
small work called " *The Psalter of Solomon.*"
This is a collection of eighteen hymns, which have
been evidently composed on the model of the
canonical Psalms, and although in a Greek version,
as they have come down to us, are supposed by
the critics to have been originally written in
Hebrew.   Some, as Ewald, have dated them as
early as the time of the Maccabees, but the greatest
weight of opinion inclines to a later period, about
fifty years before Christ.   The wail of national
depression is distinctly heard in these hymns.   But
at the same time the spirit of the Pharisee breathes

in them. Although they were composed after the heat of the great struggle was over, they bear traces of the patriotic uprising of the second century. But the most remarkable feature of these strains is their Messianic character. In the eleventh Psalm there is an anticipation of the kingdom of Messiah. In the seventeenth and eighteenth, there is a prolonged description of the .hope of Israel, and how it will be realised. , The following particulars may be gathered from this poetic language. The expected Messiah was to be a King of the House of David; He is the Son of David. He will come at a time of which God alone knows, and He will reign as a King over Israel. In character He will be perfect, a righteous King who is taught of God. In the Greek version, it is remarkable that the language should correspond exactly with that of the Septuagint—for the name of the expected King is said to be Christ the Lord (χριστὸς κύριος) (cf. LXX. Lam. iv. 20). Another striking element in the description is the absolute purity ascribed to the Messiah. "He is pure from sin" and is able to banish sinners by His Word. "Never in His days will He be infirm towards His God, since God renders Him strong in the Holy Ghost, wise in counsel, with might and righteousness. The blessing of the Lord being upon

Him, He does not fail. This is the beauty of the King of Israel, whom God hath chosen, to set Him over the house of Israel, to rule it. Thus invincible, not by outward might, but in His God, He will bring His people the blessings of restoration to their tribal possessions and of righteousness, but break in pieces His enemies, not by outward weapons, but by the word of His mouth, purify Jerusalem, and judge the nations, who will be subject to His rule, and behold and own His glory" (see especially Psalm xvii. vers. 25, 35, 36, 41, 43, 47). Ewald thinks that these striking Psalms were certainly the work of a single poet. "Amid the ashes of the Messianic hopes, which had slumbered for centuries, they were kindled anew with the most marvellous glow, and in not adducing the utterances of similar expectations at an earlier date, these songs do but testify to the greater purity and force which mark the inwardness and warmth of the resurrection of these hopes as they are presented here. On the whole, the songs are certainly, in many passages, only an echo of various pieces in the Old Testament, and their beauty simply consists in their great simplicity and sincerity; but they afford the most striking evidence of the vigour with which much that was finest and most lasting in the contents of

L

the Old Testament was striving to reappear in outward life." These remarks of the critic, which are made on the supposition that the book dates about a century and a half before Christ, have still greater force if the time of its publication must be placed a century later—for the political degeneracy of the nation proceeded at a rapid rate, and after the introduction of the Romans on the scene, and the taking of Jerusalem by Pompey, it is very full of significance that there should be a writer capable of so much genuine Old Testament feeling; calling upon his contemporaries to recognise that their sufferings were due to their violation of the covenant and their departure from the true standard of Judaism, and pointing to the Hope of Messiah as the one true consolation of Israel, to which all were invited to cling.

We have some direct evidence in addition to the language of this book, the Psalter of Solomon, in the character ascribed to Anna, the prophetess, and the aged Simeon, in the reference made to them in St. Luke's Gospel (ii. 25–38). Anna had attended for eighty years in the Temple with fasting and prayer, waiting for the appearance of the Messiah. We cannot doubt that there were, as we shall see in a later chapter, in Judea at least, a number of faithful souls who were imbued with the same expectation. Josephus himself acknowledges that, for years before the destruction of Jerusalem, such a state of mind was widespread in the nation. Why should we not regard the Psalter of Solomon as proceeding from such a remnant of the people, actuated by a lively faith, and encouraging one another to find in their ancient Scriptures the hope which they could not find in their external condition ? No doubt there were great differences among those who entertained such expectations. Some were mere political zealots and dreamers, others were deeply religious students of the Word of God and Israelites indeed, like Nathaniel; but the evidence of the fact that the nation was pervaded with the Messianic idea is not invalidated by the signs of division and separation between the true and the false Israel. We must notice, therefore, before leaving this subject, the language of the Rabbinical writers, much of which, no doubt, was written down after the Christian era, but none the less bearing witness to the state of mind which prevailed before the advent of Messiah.

It has already been observed that the Targums or Chaldee paraphrases are, for the most part, of later date than the New Testament. That of Onkelos, however, which is on the Pentateuch, is now generally admitted to be before our era ; that of Jonathan

is not very much later.   The familiar passages in
the Old Testament, which we are accustomed to
apply to the Messiah, were plainly so interpreted
by the Jews themselves at that time, as, *e.g.*, Gen.
iii. 15 : "It shall bruise thy head, and thou shalt
bruise his heel;" Gen. xlix. 10 : "The sceptre shall
not depart from Judah, nor a lawgiver from between
his feet, until Shiloh come."   Modern Jews would
fain interpret the word "sceptre" as meaning rod of
chastisement, that is, that Judah shall be punished
for rebellion until Shiloh come ; but both Onkelos
and Jonathan, and the Jerusalem Targum in addition, confirm the Christian view.   The prophecy of
Balaam (Numb. xxiv. 17) is thus rendered by Onkelos : "A king shall rise out of the house of Jacob,
and the Messiah shall be accounted out of the house
of Israel, who shall rule over all the sons of men."
Targum Jonathan is substantially the same.   Maimonides says : " A sceptre shall rise out of Israel,
this is the King Messiah, and shall smite the corners
of Moab; this is David, as it is written (2 Sam.
viii. 2), And he smote Moab, &c.   And He shall
bear rule over the children of Seth ; this is the
King Messiah, of whom it is written (Psalm lxxii.
8), He shall have dominion from sea to sea, and
from the river to the ends of the earth (Tract,
Melakin, chap. xi. sect. 1)."   The same coincidence

between the Christian and Jewish interpretations may be seen in such passages as Isaiah ix. 6, 7; xi., lii., liii.; Micah v. 2; Psalms ii., xiv., lxxii.; and other instances might be easily adduced. It has been remarked, as a proof of the general application of such passages to the Messiah by the Jews of the time preceding the Christian era, that works which came from the Rabbinical school after the appearance of the Gospels rather exalted than lowered the conception of Messiah's dignity. Had such views been inconsistent with the traditional ideas they would certainly not have been published. What the prevailing ideas were we may see from such a work as the Apocalypse of Baruch, published about 100 A.D., or from the Fourth Book of Esdras (2 Esdras in the Apocrypha). The Rabbis said, in the Midrash on Prov. viii. 9, that there were seven things created before the world—the Throne of Glory, Messiah, the King, the Thorah, ideal Israel, the Temple, Repentance, and Gehenna. "In the Talmud," says Dr. Edersheim, "it is not only implied that the Messiah may already be among the living, but a strange story is related, according to which He had actually been born in the royal palace at Bethlehem, bore the name of the Comforter, was discovered by one Rabbi Judan by a peculiar device, but had been carried away by a

storm.   Similarly, the Babylon Talmud represents
Him as sitting at the gate of Imperial Rome.   In
general, the idea of the Messiah's appearance and
concealment is familiar to Jewish tradition." There
are many passages which teach the pre-existence
and the premundane existence of Messiah, that He
should subdue Satan, and cast him into hell.   The
life and work of Moses is taken as typical of that
of the Messiah, and it is declared that He would
be "greater than the Patriarchs, higher than Moses,
and even loftier than the ministering angels." The
teaching of the Rabbis was the teaching of the synagogue.   We cannot doubt that what was inserted
in the Talmud, though exaggerated in language,
was regarded as representing the tradition of preceding ages.   The Jewish Church was filled with
the expectation of Messiah.   Those who rejected
altogether the Christian facts did not dare to meet
them with the bold denial that they corresponded
with Old Testament predictions.   Rather they set
over against the cross of Christ, which condemned
the Rabbinical spirit, the old views which they
would not admit had been proved erroneous by
the history of their people, and which would yet
be vindicated by a future manifestation of the true
Messiah.

There was a sceptical school, no doubt, among

the Jews, and there were worldly-minded men like Josephus, who made light of the ancient prophecies, but they did not represent the strict and devout Scribes—rather they were those who came under the influence of foreign nations, and resigned the exalted hope of their fathers for the sake of sordid advantages and the favour of princes.

The language of Josephus (Jewish War, bk. vi. chap. v.) is itself his condemnation, for that any intelligent reader of the Old Testament should so speak of Messianic hopes plainly proves that he is either wilfully blind or culpably ignorant. "There was an ambitious prophecy," he says, "found in the Sacred Books, that about those times One shall arise out of their own borders and put the whole world under His obedience. Which they, indeed, applied as peculiar to themselves, and several wise men were deceived in the gloss they put upon the passages. For the prophecy meant no more than Vespasian's empire, who was declared emperor in Judea." Josephus would have his readers believe that the Jews founded their hopes on a single prediction. He was writing to please the powers that were, and he knew that he was misrepresenting the Old Testament. There were some, however, who, without being corrupt and degenerate, like Josephus, were yet sophisticated by the influence

of heathen speculation and an attempt to accommodate the ideas of Judaism to the current philosophy
of the world.   By their exceptional position they
enable us to see all the more distinctly that the
strict Jews of Palestine were still, even though
unintentionally so, witnesses to the Divine idea
embodied in their nation.   The light which glowed
on the horizon of the Jewish Church foretold the
rising of the Sun of Righteousness.

CHAPTER IX.

THE JEWISH SANHEDRIM.

IN studying the state of the Jewish Church during the period which intervened between the close of the Scripture canon and the coming of our Lord Jesus Christ, one of the most suggestive and helpful facts is the rise of *The Jewish Sanhedrim*. This great council or court was certainly in existence at the time of Christ, but it was by no means what it had been at previous periods. It was shorn of much of its power. The claims which it put forth are obscure; and beyond the fact that it could be called together, and in an emergency sought to exercise something like its former jurisdiction, we are not able to ascertain much. Whether the power of life and death was ever, properly speaking, in the hands of the council, as a council, we can scarcely decide. The reference to such a power, as no longer legally claimed, may have been a wilful confusion, in the language of the Scribes and Pharisees, between the judicial powers of ancient

times and the supposed identification of the Sanhedrim with the Courts of Justice. No doubt such
powers had been exercised by the Sanhedrim, but
it was at a time when they were mere creatures of
heathen rulers, who would put their own agents
at their head.

We have already, in another place, referred to
the tradition which existed among the Jews, that
Ezra called together a number of learned and
devout men to assist him in his work of religious
and national reformation. They were called *The
Great Synagogue.* Simon the Just is said to have
been the last of that body, the meetings of which
would probably cease when the condition of Palestine became politically unfavourable to them. It is
impossible to trace the links of connection between
such a body and the Sanhedrim. There is no
evidence that any decisions were placed on record
or that any meetings were held after the time of
Malachi. But there would naturally be occasions
when the leading men in Jerusalem would be called
together for deliberation, and there is some reference to such occasions to be found in the Books of
the Maccabees (2 Macc. i. 10), "*the Council*," "*the
Senate*" (cf. iv. 44; xi. 27). The word "*Sanhedrim*" is not the word employed in these references,
but Γερουσια. It was not necessarily a religious

body of which the historian speaks. The name
"*Sanhedrim*," although it is formed after the
Hebrew, is certainly nothing else than the ordinary
Greek word Συνέδριον, and the fact that the Rabbis,
notwithstanding their desire to give ancient prestige to the Sanhedrim, have been unable to derive
the name from any Hebrew word, clearly proves
that it had its origin in the Greek period, and probably, as a distinct assembly, did not exist before
200 B.C. It is an attested fact (see Livy xiv. 32)
that the Macedonian name for such a council was
"*Sunedroin*," which became "*Sanhedrim*" among
the Jews.

But the Rabbinical writers have done their best
to connect their council with precedents which have
Scripture authority. The miserable failure of such
an attempt is sufficient evidence of the lack of historical authority. Had it been possible to trace
the antecedents of the Sanhedrim, no doubt we
should have found them in the Talmud, but instead
of that we have passages adduced out of the Pentateuch, which every most superficial reader can see
have no relevance whatever to the subject. One
passage referred to is Exodus xviii. 24–26, the
appointment of judges over Israel by Moses at the
suggestion of Jethro. Another is Deuteronomy
xvii. 9, where the command is "Thou shalt come

unto the priests, the Levites, and unto the judge that shall be in those days, and inquire." In Hilchoth Mamrim (chap. i. 1) we read, "The Great Council in Jerusalem is the foundation-stone of the Oral Law and the pillars of the doctrine; and from them the statute and the judgment go forth to all Israel. They have the warrant of the Law, for it is said, 'According to the sentence of the Law which they shall teach thee,' &c.; which is an affirmative precept, and every one who believes in Moses, our master, and in his Law, is bound to rest the practice of the Law on them, and to lean on them." The other passage on which great stress is laid is Numbers xi. 16, the appointment by Moses of the seventy elders. Hilchoth Sanhedrim, ch. i. 2, "How many councils (or tribunals) ought to be established in Israel, and of how many members ought they to consist? *Ans.* The great council in the Temple called the Great Sanhedrim ought to be established first, and the number of its members ought to be seventy-one; for it is said, 'Gather unto me seventy men of the elders of Israel;' and to them Moses is to be added, as it is said, 'And they shall stand there with thee.' This makes seventy-one."

In the same work we read, "A king is not to be appointed except by the decision of the Great

Council of Seventy-one. The minor councils through the tribes and towns are not to be established except by the Council of Seventy-one. Judgment is not to be passed on a tribe that has been entirely seduced, nor upon a false prophet, nor upon a high priest in capital cases, except by the Great Council. (In mere money matters the tribunal of three is competent.) In like manner an elder is not declared rebellious, nor a city dealt with as seduced, nor the water-bitters administered to the suspected adulteress, except by the Great Council. Neither is an addition made to the city nor to the courts. Neither are armies led forth to the wars of permission; nor the elders led forth to measure in case of a slain person (Deut. xxi. 1, &c.), except by command of the Great Council, for it is said, 'Every great matter they shall bring to thee'" (Exod. xviii. 22). The reasoning by which the Rabbis try to support the authority of the Sanhedrim, and so of the Oral Law, is nothing better than a tissue of absurdities and falsehoods. In one case they suppose a person living in the time of Moses to be also living in the time of David. And they leap one great period of two hundred years without pretending to prove that there was any council in existence. But it may be admitted that there probably were some lingering remains of the

Great Synagogue in the Greek period, and that the
assembly spoken of in the first Book of Maccabees,
which conferred the supreme power on Simon,
father of John Hyrcanus, was the same council
that was subsequently styled the Sanhedrim. "At
Saramel in the Great Congregation of the priests
and people and rulers of the nation and elders of
the country were these things notified unto us."
So was it written on the tables of brass set upon
pillars in Mount Zion, after Simon had confirmed
his league with the Roman Senate. There are
coins on which the Sanhedrim is described as the
Chebber or Senate of the Jews. John Hyrcanus
was Greek in his sympathies, and adopted the title
'Ιουδα βασιλεύς. His successor, Alexander Jannæus,
quarrelled with the leading party among the Jews,
who were Pharisees, but on his death-bed recom-
mended his wife Salome to trust true Pharisees;
while she avoided the painted ones. Salome accordingly gave them such privileges during her
reign of nine years that they ultimately ventured
to summon her son Hyrcanus II. before their
tribunal. It was on that occasion that the name
"*Sanhedrim*" was first given. Previous to that
time, whatever council there was, was not called
by the Greek name, but by the Jewish, the Great
Synagogue or the House of Judgment (*Beth Din*).

In the days of Herod we find a notice of the Sanhedrim which shows that they had little real power, though still the show of it. In the year 47 B.C., Herod, who was then governor of Galilee, had ventured to put to death some Jewish robbers, and was called before the council that he might be rebuked for his presumption. Hyrcanus, the ruling high priest, as the president of the council, yielded to the entreaties of the mothers of the victims and summoned the offender before the Sanhedrim. Josephus tells us that Herod appeared surrounded with armed men, and that Sextus, the prefect of Syria, sent a letter to Hyrcanus calling upon him to renounce the trial. The Sanhedrim therefore dismissed him without pronouncing any punishment on his crimes. "One of the council, Samœus, told them plainly that they would repent of their leniency, and when Herod had fixed himself in the kingdom he slew every one presiding in this court, nay, and Hyrcanus himself, but excepted Samœus, who, for his extraordinary moderation and justice, he held in great honour, and because when Herod and Sextus laid siege to Jerusalem he was the only person who admonished the citizens to receive Herod, representing that as they were so very wicked it was next to an impossibility to escape falling into his power." The judges in the Sanhedrim were exceedingly mortified that Herod escaped, but we may see in the whole occurrence a proof that their power was already gone, and that henceforth they would confine their attention almost entirely to ecclesiastical matters. (See Joseph. Antiq. xiv. 9.)

It is, however, to the influence of the Sanhedrim on the religious views of the people, and its connection with the growth of Rabbinical opinion, that we must now turn. It seems probable that the extreme arrogance of their tone, as the assumed teachers and authorised religious rulers, was the quite late development of the fifty years immediately preceding our Lord, when the purer spirit of the patriotic Asmoneans had died out and the Pharisaic party had degenerated into a school of self-righteous dogmatists and ritualists. It was about the time of Herod that the title *"Rabbi"* came into use, a lengthened form of the title *"Rab,"* which no doubt was adopted from the old Hebrew or Chaldee, meaning chief or prince, and was common in compound words, as we see in Rabshakeh, Rabmag, Rabsaris, &c. The application of such a term to religious teachers points to the usurpation of authority and political power by the Sanhedrim. There were two chief officers in the council, *the President* and *the Vice-President.*

The latter was the "*Father of the House of Judgment*," *i.e.*, the president over that portion of the council which sat as a court in ordinary cases. The chief man, however, was called *the Prince*, or "*Nasi*," and the fact that the council had two heads, or presidents, led to the distinction of schools which subsequently arose. Each head gathered round him a number of followers, who gave special heed to his judgments and upheld his authority. It is on the ground of these appointments that the later Rabbis endeavour to place the authority of their tradition. They carry back the line of eminent teachers as far as Simon the Just. He delivered the tradition to Antigonus of Socho. Antigonus of Socho handed it on to Joses Ben Joezer and Joseph Ben Jochanan, which were the first of the "*couples.*" After that time they set forth a succession of "*couples*," although they are quite unable to make out a chronological order. We have Joshua Ben Perachiah and Nathan the Arbelite, Simeon Ben Shetach and Jehuah Ben Tabbai, Shemaiah and Abtalion; Hillel and Shammai. Shemaiah and Abtalion are said to have been proselytes and brothers, descended from Sennacherib, King of Assyria, by an Israelite woman, and to have perished in the great slaughter

M

of the Sanhedrim, perpetrated by Herod in revenge
for their severity towards him.

A great gap of more than a hundred years is found
between those men of the time of Herod and their
predecessors of the time of the Maccabees, plainly
showing that the line of succession is a mere fabrication previous to the time of Hillel and Shammai.
Josephus (Ant. xiv. 9, 4) refers to two men, Pollio
and Sammœas, whom some have identified with
Abtalion and Shemaiah, others with Hillel and
Shammai. It seems as though *Abtalion* was a
mythical personage, and was really identical with
Hillel. At all events, we can certify that *Hillel*
and *Shammai* were the two presidents of the
council in the time of Herod. *Hillel* is said to
have been descended, on his mother's side, from
King David, through Shephatiah, the son of Abital,
David's wife. He was an eminently learned man,
and is placed by the Rabbis in the chief place of
their ancient authority. For forty years he was
president of the Sanhedrim, and was succeeded by
his lineal descendants in the same offices, amongst
whom were *Simeon*, who took the infant Jesus into
his arms in the Temple and sung his "*Nunc
Dimittis*," and *Gamaliel*, at whose feet the Apostle
Paul sat, and before whom, as President, the
apostles were summoned (Acts v. 34). "*Gamaliel*

the old" he was called, because he survived to the eighteenth year before the destruction of Jerusalem. A descendant of Hillel, *Rabbi Judah Hakkadosh*, was the author of the Mishna. Hillel was born in Babylonia, and resided there until he was forty years old, when he removed to Jerusalem. He then devoted himself to the study of the Pentateuch, and became so eminent that at eighty years of age he was made President of the Council, living, it is said, to the extreme old age of one hundred and twenty years. Some have dated his presidency 30 B.C., but this has been probably in order to make it exactly one hundred years from the destruction of Jerusalem. The name of *Manahem* occurs in Josephus, as contemporary with Hillel. He is said to have been withdrawn by Herod's influence into court life, and been succeeded by *Shammai*, who was a scholar of Hillel. The scholar soon became the rival of the master. The followers of each disputed with those of the opposite school. They differed on many points, and some have maintained that their spirit was diverse, that Hillel was of a mild and conciliatory disposition, and that Shammai was very prejudiced and violent. In order to help their theory of authority the Rabbis have introduced the fiction of a *Divine voice from heaven*, sent to give decision

between the two disputants and their followers.
Dr. Edersheim, however, is of opinion that in both
respects scholars have been misled. "It is not
correct," he says, "to describe Hillel as consistently
the more liberal and mild. The teaching of both
was supposed to have been declared by the 'Voice
from heaven' (the *Bath-Kol*), as 'the words of the
living God;' yet the Law was to be henceforth
according to the teaching of Hillel."

Dr. Stanley has given an interesting account of
Hillel, though it rests only on tradition. "Like
Ezra, to whom his countrymen often compared
him, Hillel belonged to the vast Babylonian settle-
ment. Unlike Ezra, he was not of the priestly
class; but like One who was shortly to come after
him, descended from the house of David; and, like
that other One, a humble workman, drawn to Jerusalem only by the thirst for 'hearing and asking
questions.' He came with his brother Shebna,
and worked for the scanty remuneration of half a
denarius, the coin known in Latin as '*victoriatus*,'
in Greek as '*tropaicon*,' from the figure of the
goddess Victory upon it. This he divided between
the pay for his lodgings and the pay to the doorkeeper of the school where Shemaiah and Abtalion
taught. On a certain occasion, when he had failed
in his work, the churlish doorkeeper would not let

him enter. It was the eve of the Sabbath, there were no lights stirring, and he took advantage of the darkness to climb to the window-sill to listen. It was a winter night, and the listening youth was first benumbed and then buried three cubits deep under a heavy snowfall. As the day dawned, Shemaiah turned to his colleague and said, 'Dear brother Abtalion, why is our school so dark this morning?' They turned to the window and found it darkened by a motionless human form, enveloped in the snowflakes. They brought him down, bathed, rubbed him with oil, placed him before the fire—in short, broke for his sake their Sabbatical repose, saying, 'Surely he must be worth a violation of the Sabbath!' He was, in regard to the traditionary lore, what Ezra was supposed to have been in regard to the written Law. He it was who collected and codified the floating maxims which guided the schools" (iii. 447).

In an interesting excursus to his "Life of Christ," Archdeacon Farrar gives several of the Rabbinical stories about Hillel, which, however, must be received with the utmost caution. We cannot even accept the general tone of them as indicating the breadth or mildness of Hillel as a teacher, for there can be no doubt at all that the Rabbis were greatly influenced by Christian senti-

ments, being desirous of proving that their great
Rabbi, who preceded Jesus of Nazareth, was the
source of all that was good in the Saviour's doctrine.   The school of Hillel was the majority, and
Dr. Edersheim thinks that "generally only one side
of his character has been presented by writers, and
even this in greatly exaggerated language.   His
much-lauded gentleness, peacefulness, and charity,
were rather negative than positive qualities.   He
was a philosophic Rabbi, whose real interest lay
in a far other direction than that of sympathy with
the people, and whose motto seemed indeed to imply, 'We, the sages, are the people of God ; but this
people, who know not the Law, are cursed.'   The
school of Hillel, which henceforth commanded the
majority, were men of no political colour, theological theorists, self-seeking jurists, vain rather
than ambitious.   The two schools of the Hillelites
and the Shammaites were violently opposed and
on occasion came to blows."

It is difficult, says Dr. Edersheim, to ascertain
what occurred, but the Shammaites had the majority
of votes, and eighteen decrees were passed in which
the two schools agreed, eighteen questions were
carried by a majority, and eighteen remained undecided.   "In general, the tendency of these
eighteen decrees was of a most violently anti-

Gentile, intolerant, and exclusive character. Yet such value was attached to them, that while any other decree of the sages might be altered by a more grave, learned, and authoritative assembly, these eighteen decrees might not, under any circumstances, be modified" (ii. 14). "Although the school of Hillel was supposed in general to make the yoke lighter, and that of Shammai heavier, yet not only did they agree on many points, but the school of Hillel was not unfrequently even more strict than that of his rival. (Twenty-four points are mentioned.) In truth, their differences seem often only prompted by a spirit of opposition, so that the serious business of religion became in their hands one of rival authority and mere wrangling. (Many, very many of these are so utterly trivial and absurd, that only the hair-splitting ingenuity of theologians can account for them; others so profane that it is difficult to understand how any religion could co-exist with them" (vol. ii. p. 407).

The remarks of Dr. Stanley may be placed beside these, and the more favourable view which he gives of Hillel will be received the more carefully as it is seen to be modified by that of Jewish scholars. "At first sight, as we turn the dreary pages of the Mishna, there seems to be little to choose be-

tween Hillel and Shammai. Their disputes turn,
for the most part, on points so infinitely little that
the small controversies of ritual and dogma which
have vexed the soul of Christendom, seem great in
comparison. They are worth recording only as
accounting for the obscurity into which they have
fallen, and also because Churches of all ages and
creeds may be instructed by the reflection that
questions of the mode of eating and cooking,
and walking and sitting, seemed as important to
the teachers of Israel—on the eve of their nation's
destruction, and of the greatest religious revolution
that the world has seen—as the questions of dress
or posture, or modes of appointment, or verbal
formulas, have seemed to contending schools of
Christian theology. But in the darkness of the
Rabbinical schools of Palestine, Hillel was, as it
were, the morning star of the bright dawn that was
rising in the hills of Galilee. It has been reserved
for modern times to recognise this extraordinary
merit. The teacher over whom both Josephus and
Eusebius pass without word, saw further than any
other man of his generation into the heart and
essence of religion. In him the freedom, the elevation, the latitude which had breathed through the
poetic imagery and grand idealism of the psalmists
and prophets in the days of the higher inspirations

of Judaism, now expressed themselves for the first time in the direct practical maxims of what we may call the modern thought of the Herodian, the Augustan age. Even amidst the trivial casuistry and ceremonial etiquettes which furnish the materials for the larger part of Hillel's decisions, they lean, not indeed invariably, but as a general rule, to the more liberal and spiritual side, and they encourage the rights of the congregation and the nation as against the claims of a grasping sacerdotal caste. And even when he appeared to submit, he introduced, if he did not create, a logical process by which, under a peculiar name acquired in his hands (Prosbol), he contrived to minimise the stringent effects, not only of the tradition, but of the Law itself. But there are sayings which tower not only far above those questions of tithes, anise, and cummin, into the weightier matters of the Law, but above the merely presidential aphorisms of the earlier Rabbis, and which must have created around them an atmosphere not only in which they themselves could live and be appreciated, but which must have rendered more possible both the origination and the acceptance of any other sayings of a kindred nature in that other coming age. " Be gentle as Hillel and not harsh as Shammai," was the proverb which marked the

final estimate of the latitudinarian compared with
the rigorist teacher, when the spirit of partisanship
had cooled before the calmer judgment of posterity.
Two practical sayings alone have survived of the
sterile teaching of Shammai. " Let thy repetition
of the law be at a fixed hour," was the hard and
fast line by which his disciples were to be bound
down, as by an inexorable necessity, to the punc-
tual reading of the Sacred Book, as of a breviary,
at hours never to be lost sight of. " Speak little
and do much, but do what thou hast to do with a
cheerful countenance." That voice has a touching
accent, as though he felt that the frequent profes-
sions and austere demeanour which were congenial
to his natural disposition might perchance prove a
stumbling-block to the cause which was dear to
him. But when from these " scrannel pipes " of
Shammai we turn to his less popular but more
deeply beloved rival, we find ourselves listening
to strains of a far higher mood. " Be of Aaron's
disciples, who loved peace, pursued peace, loved all
creatures, and attracted them towards the Law."
Although not a priest himself, and by his position
thrown into antagonism to the order, he yet had
the rare merit of seeing in an ancient institution
the better side of its traditions and its capabilities,
and of commending it to his countrymen. " He

who makes his own name famous, and does not increase in wisdom, shall perish. He who learns nothing is as though he has done something worthy of death. He who makes a profit of the crowning glory of a teacher's place, away with him!" This represents the religious passion for mental improvement—the sacred duty of diligence, which carries within it the stimulus of all modern science, the true ideal of the "scholar." It shows also the Socratic disinterestedness in imparting knowledge transplanted into a sphere where it will give birth to one of the most striking characteristics of a future apostle. "If I am not mine own, who is mine? Yet, if I am mine own, what am I? And if not now, when?" It is one of those enigmas in which, from the time of Solomon downwards, the Jewish sages delighted, yet full of deep meaning. It expresses the threefold mission placed before the human soul—the call to absolute independence, the worthlessness of selfish isolation, the necessity of immediate exertion to fortify the one and to correct the other. "Had Hillel," says Ewald, "left us but this single saying, we should be for ever grateful to him, for scarce anything can be said more briefly, more profoundly, or more earnestly." A heathen came to Shammai, and begged to be taught the whole Law while he stood

on one foot. Shammai, indignant at the thought
that the Law could be taught so simply and so
shortly, drove him forth with the staff which he
held in his hand. The Gentile went to Hillel, who
accepted him, and said, "What thou wouldst not
thyself, do not to thy neighbour. This is the
whole Law, and its application is, Go and do this!
Wish not to be better than the whole community,
nor be confident of thyself till the day of thy death.
Think not of anything that it will not be heard, for
heard at last it surely will be ; think not that thou
canst calculate on the time when thou shalt have
anything, for how easily will it come to pass that
thou shalt never have it at all. The more meat
at his banquets a man hath, so much the more
is the food for worms ; the more wealth he hath,
so much the more care ; the more wives, so much
the more opening for superstition ; the more maid-
servants, so much the more temptation to license ;
the more slaves, so much the more room for plunder.
But the more of Law, so much the more of life ;
the more of schools, so much the more of wisdom ;
the more of counsel, so much the more of insight ;
the more of righteousness, so much the more of
peace. If a man gains a good name he gains it for
himself alone; if he gains a knowledge of the Law,
it is for eternal life." These are maxims which are

more than philosophical, they are almost Apostolical.

Dr. Stanley has, however, followed too implicitly the views of Ewald and others of the Germans, and it must be remembered that much which is reported of Hillel has come to us through the Rabbinical traditions, and cannot be received except with the greatest reserve, especially as it was the deliberate aim of the post-Christian Rabbis to set off Hillel in opposition to Jesus, in which they have been too much followed by the rationalistic school of Germany. As Dr. Farrar has observed—"Hillel was undoubtedly a great and good man, and he deserved the wail uttered over his grave—'Ah, the gentle, the holy, the scholar of Ezra;' but to compare his teaching with that of the Saviour is absurd. It was legal, casuistic, and narrow, while that of Jesus was religious, moral, and human. Let any candid reader consult the translation of the Talmudic treatise *Berachoth*, by M. Schwab, and see the kind of miserably minute questions of infinitely little matters of formalism which occupied the mind and life of Hillel, and calmly consider the mixture of scorn and pity with which Jesus would have treated the notion that there was in such questions any intrinsic importance. He will then be able to judge for himself of the folly and untenability of the statement that Hillel was the true master of Jesus" ("Life of Christ," vol. ii. p. 460).

At the same time, making all abatement from the exaggerated views of the Rabbis, it may be admitted that there appeared in the Sanhedrim, towards the end of the period between the last of the prophets and the advent of our Saviour, something like a new spirit, a spirit of dissatisfaction with the dead legalism of the past hundred years, and a craving after a higher teaching and a freer life. There was no room for such a spirit to expand itself and grow into a living power in Judaism so long as it was confined within the limits of Rabbinical tradition. Hence it was that He who came to set His people free, and open the gate of righteousness to the world, was not a Rabbi, did not teach as a so-called "Master in Israel;" but, on the other hand, received His appointment directly from God, by the baptism of the Holy Ghost, and distinctly opposed His spiritual doctrine to that which had been "said by them of old time." The light which was in the Jewish Sanhedrim was turned into darkness. But the night passed away, and the True Light shone forth in the "Teacher come from God," who did not "*destroy the Law*" by the subtleties of a self-righteous pedantry, but fulfilled it by the gracious freedom and inexhaustible sufficiency of the Spirit of Truth, the Spirit of Light and Love, cleansing, purifying, renewing and saving, bringing forth the true Israel out of the old, the new Jerusalem, coming down out of heaven from God.

CHAPTER X.

PHILO OF ALEXANDRIA.

WE are now drawing near, in our view of the Jewish Church, the close of that long period which separates the last of the prophets, Malachi, from the advent of the Saviour. We have already described the character of that remarkable revival of Jewish sentiment and faith which was identified with the patriotic efforts of the Maccabees, and which continued for some time to animate the religious life of Palestine. But in proportion as this religious revival was overshadowed by political disorder and depression, it changed its character and became a narrow Rabbinism, which robbed Judaism more and more of its best features, and cut it off from intercourse with surrounding nations. The resource of despairing patriots, in the land of their fathers, lay in the wild dreams of a Messianic revelation, in which it was hoped the zeal and devotedness of the strictest Jews would be rewarded, and the Law of Moses, as interpreted by the Rabbis, would be made the Law of the world. There had grown up, however, during the last two centuries, another form of Jewish life, which, chiefly through the influence of one remarkable man, was henceforth destined to a great place in the future religious history of the world. Alexandria had its Jewish nation, almost a nation to itself, in contrast with that in Palestine. Ever since the Ptolemies had favoured the Jews, and their Scriptures were translated into Greek, the intercourse between the more learned and wealthy among them and the Gentiles, with whom they were compelled to associate, had been breaking down prejudice and enlarging their views. The intellectual life of Alexandria was based upon the principle of Eclecticism. The situation of Egypt was favourable to the cultivation of a cosmopolitan spirit. East and West there came into contact, and freely mingled together. The magnificent Library with its neighbouring School was the meeting-place of Jew and Gentile, European and Asiatic, men of profound thought, and men of active business talent, and the Jew could scarcely resist for long the influence of such an atmosphere. He began to philosophise himself, as his neighbours did, although his nation had never encouraged philosophical studies; he began to read his Scriptures with a view to find

N

in them the decisions of Divine authority on the questions which were being agitated in the School. The result was the rise of what was subsequently called " *Hellenism*," a compromise between the strict Judaism of Palestine and the broader spirit of Greek religion and philosophy. It was in no sense a renunciation of the claims which the Jewish people preserved among them to superiority over the world. It was not a lowering of Scripture authority. But it was an attempt to accommodate Judaism to the new circumstances in which it was placed in Egypt, by calling in all that Gentile philosophy and culture could afford to unfold and develop the hidden treasures of the Old Testament. The chief representative of this *new Judaism*, for such it should be called, was the Alexandrian Philo, born probably about 20 B.C., and a man who, both by his great wealth and high social position, and by his extraordinary intellectual power, might be regarded as the leading Jew of that great and flourishing Hebrew colony.

We have already referred to the works of a much earlier Alexandrian, *Aristobulus*. We find that the Jews of Palestine in their time of distress and danger, sent a letter to " Aristobulus, master of King Ptolemy, and of the stock of the anointed priests" (2 Macc. i. 9). This Ptolemy was Ptolemy VII., or Philometor, and there was probably a "*Judas*" who became his instructor and was named "*Aristobulus*," a man of great learning, who, with others, such as Demetrius, Eupolemus, Artapanus, Cleodemus, Jason, and others like them, laboured to bring Jewish views into closer union with Greek thought and literature. Aristobulus flourished about 180 B.C. His chief work was entitled "*Explanations of the Mosaic Law.*" "His object," says Ewald, "was, before the eyes of the king himself, to dissipate certain prejudices against the Law. The fragments which remain prove the work to have been the composition of a refined mind; and in the treatment of such questions as how arms, face, and feet could be ascribed to God in the Holy Scriptures, how the descent of God on to Sinai in fire and other symbols of the same nature were to be understood, how God could have rested on the seventh day—we observe, in fact, the earliest and tenderest attempt at connected allegorical explanation placed as far as possible on a philosophical basis." There were other works besides those of Aristobulus which aimed at the same reconciliation between Gentile philosophy and Jewish religion. But this allegorical method of interpretation was not applied very extensively to the Old Testament until the time of Philo. In considering, however, the sources from which he drew in his writings, it is important to keep before us the two Books of the Apocrypha, to which allusion has been already made, and which certainly preceded Philo in time, the Book of *Ecclesiasticus* or The Wisdom of the Son of Sirach, and the Book of *The Wisdom of Solomon*—the former, perhaps, dating as early as the time of Aristobulus, and the latter certainly composed before the time of Herod, and probably published eighty years before the birth of Philo. We must briefly describe the teaching of these books as introductory to our notice of Philo's doctrine, as he seems to have freely used them.

In *Ecclesiasticus*, which was originally composed in Hebrew and afterwards translated into Greek, the aim of the translator was to adapt the work of an enlightened and devout Jew of a former period to the people of Alexandria, to commend to them Jewish doctrine and practical maxims. It is not an attempt to harmonise Greek thought and Jewish theology, for it is thoroughly Jewish throughout, but rather to select that which was best in the Old Testament and commend it to the attention of the Gentiles. It begins with proverbs, wise sayings, full of practical sagacity, and applying to the whole extent of human life. These are followed by a higher strain, in which wisdom is regarded as not a mere regulation of common life, but as a Divine gift for all nations. "We possess in this work," says Ewald, "the finest composition in continuation of the Psalms which the Apocryphal books contain. The whole style is more artistic ; single maxims are often extremely pointed ; the language is full of images and flowers, and while the writer seeks to describe with great detail the whole compass of morality, he depicts certain special moral relations with peculiar ease (as in the proverbs about slaves, Ecclus. xxxiii. 24–31)." The conclusion, in which the heroic men of Israel are celebrated, and which is highly poetical, is full of intense national feeling, and yet, at the same time, is intended to attract the Greek world by its spirit of hero-worship. There is also, in chapter xliii., a very beautiful description of the glory of the natural world, and an invitation to see God in it and above it. "When ye glorify the Lord, exalt Him as much as ye can ; for even yet will He far exceed ; and when ye exalt Him, put forth all your strength and be not weary ; for ye can never go far enough. Who hath seen Him that he might tell us ? and who can magnify Him as He is ? There are yet hid greater things than

these be, for we have seen but a few of His works.
For the Lord hath made all things, and to the
godly hath He given wisdom" (vers. 30–33).
But the portion of this interesting work to which
Philo would be most indebted, is the twenty-fourth
chapter in praise of wisdom.   Here we plainly per-
ceive a recollection of the language of the Book of
Proverbs, but, at the same time, the personification
of wisdom is carried out with more detail, and
here and there are traces of an Alexandrian style
of thought.   "I came out of the mouth of the
Most High, and covered the earth as a cloud.   I
dwell in high places, and my throne is in a cloudy
pillar.   I alone compassed the circuit of heaven,
and walked in the bottom of the deep.   In the
waves of the sea, and in all the earth, and in every
people and nation I got a possession.   With all
these I sought not : and in whose inheritance shall
I abide ?"   The answer to this question plainly
declares that the True Wisdom is laid up in Zion,
but all are invited to receive it.   " I will yet make
doctrine to shine as the morning, and will send her
light afar off.   I will yet pour out doctrine as prophecy, and leave it to all ages for ever.   Behold
that I have not laboured for myself only, but for
all them that seek wisdom " (vers. 32–34).   There
is no compromise of Judaism in this book, but

there is an evident desire to call in the world to a participation in Divine blessings.

The Wisdom of Solomon is a much more philosophical book than *Ecclesiasticus*; it is regarded by some as proceeding directly from the Alexandrian School, and as "the most beautiful and important of all the Hellenistic productions." The author has "steeped his mind," says Ewald, "in the principal books of the Old Testament, and there recognised the eternal foundations of all true religion with such living power that he beheld none but these pure and ever-quickening truths in all their brightness, and before this great light all its lower and imperfect elements vanished away. He had in the same way saturated himself with Greek culture, and nurtured his spirit with many thoughts and principles of the higher Greek philosophy, particularly the Platonic." The idea of the book is that the wise king, Solomon, is addressing the powers and princes of the world, and the searchers after wisdom, and he is instructing them in the Way of Life. The first six chapters are an address to the judges of the earth, an appeal to them to find true wisdom in the teaching of the Divine Spirit: "For the Spirit of the Lord filleth the world; and that which containeth all things hath knowledge of the voice" (i. 7). The great

principle which is set forth is the eternity of man :
"*For God created man to be immortal, and made
him to be an image of His own Eternity.*" "The
souls of the righteous are in the hand of God."
"Wisdom is glorious, and never fadeth away : yea,
she is easily seen of them that love her, and found
of such as seek her." "Love is the keeping of her
laws." "The desire of wisdom bringeth to a
kingdom." "If your delight be then in thrones
and sceptres, O ye kings of the people, honour
wisdom that ye may reign for evermore." Then
follows a discourse on Wisdom itself, "What she
is, and how she came up." Taking the history of
Solomon as an example of success in seeking wisdom, the writer insists on the power of prayer, and
the direct inspiration of the Spirit. There is
much in the description of wisdom which reminds
us of the language of the Schools : "If a man love
righteousness, her labours are virtues : for she
teacheth temperance and prudence, justice and
fortitude; which are such things as man can have
nothing more profitable in this life." "By means
of her I shall obtain immortality, and leave behind
me an everlasting memorial to them that come
after me." The ninth chapter is a sublime prayer,
which Solomon is supposed to have uttered, and
whereby he obtained wisdom. Then we have the

memorable instances of the great and good in former ages, all inspired of God. Adam, Noah, Abraham, Lot, Jacob, Joseph, Moses, the Israelites. Speaking of the sparing mercy of God towards mankind, we find a philosophical idea, which was common at that time, introduced, the pervading influence of the Divine Spirit in all men. "For thine incorruptible Spirit is in all things." Reference is made in the thirteenth chapter to the perverse philosophies of the heathen, how they "deemed either fire, or wind, or the swift air, or the circle of the stars, or the violent waters, or the lights of heaven, to be the gods which govern the world." "But yet for this they are the less to be blamed, for they peradventure err, seeking God, and desirous to find Him. For, being conversant in His works, they search Him diligently, and believe their sight, because the things are beautiful that are seen." In the fourteenth chapter we meet with that doctrine of the Word of God which was afterwards so fully wrought out by Philo: "Thy Word, O Lord, healeth all things." "The Word preserveth them that put their trust in Thee." It is the "*Almighty Word*" which "leaped down from heaven out of Thy royal throne as a fierce man of war, into the midst of a land of destruction," and punished the Egyptians

and all idolaters.   The book is, undoubtedly, full
of Messianic expectation, and it has been observed,
by Ewald, that it is "so far before all the other
Hellenistic productions, so abounding in words and
thoughts which remind us strikingly of the New
Testament, that it has even been attempted to
detect a Christian in its author.   He is, however,
no other than a highly inspired Jew; and in no
single case can it be proved that he derived any
one of his words or thoughts from Christianity.
Of the Law he says little, as he is engaged in
deeper contemplations; and he rises far above the
narrow-heartedness and hypocrisy of the Pharisees
into shining heights; yet it is clear that, in his
view, there is nothing holy but the contents of the
Law."   It has been suggested that the work may
have been by Philo himself, but the style is not
that of Philo, and the entire absence throughout
the book of the allegorical method, and the simple
practical directness of the appeals to the heathen
to accept the teaching of the Spirit of God, are
decided proofs that it proceeded from some other
hand.   It was from the Messianic impulse that it
came.   It is the opinion of Ewald that on that
account it cannot be dated much more than a
generation before Philo, but, at all events, it is
quite possible that at the time when he would be

writing, that is twenty or thirty years after the birth of Christ, the book would be regarded as comparatively old, some seventy or eighty years having passed away since it was given to the world, or even more. There seems a large concurrence of opinion that it dates about one hundred years before Christ, but the date of its publication remains an open question. We are now prepared to look more closely into the teaching of Philo himself, many of whose remarkable writings have been preserved to us.

Very little is known of the history of Philo. He was an Alexandrian by birth, and probably belonged to a priestly family. The only fact by which we are able to learn anything of his position in his native city is the embassy to the Roman Emperor, Caligula, in which Philo took the chief part, and which arrived in Rome in the winter of 39 A.D., lasting until the spring of the following year. Philo was then, as he tells us, an old man, being sixty years of age. The main object of the embassy was to procure the revocation of the Imperial decree requiring divine honours to be paid to the statue of the Emperor. The statue of Caligula was ordered to be set up in the Temple at Jerusalem, and would have been placed there had not the mad Emperor been called away by death

in 41 A.D. The writings of Philo which remain
to us are very various, but chiefly take the form
of commentaries on the Pentateuch. The subjects
are those which are suggested by the Scriptures.
The Doctrine of Creation, the meaning of the
Levitical Law, the Cherubim, the sacrifices of
Cain and Abel, the division of the human family
into the good and the bad, the giants, the un-
changeableness of God, the incidents in the life of
Noah, drunkenness, the Confusion of Languages,
the Migration of Abraham, the Wise Man as
typified in Abraham, the Statesman as typified in
Joseph, Moses, his office and his institutions, the
Monarchy, Special Laws of the Jews, the Sacred
Festivals, Justice and Magistrates. These are
some of the subjects which Philo finds in the
Pentateuch, and on which he treats. Then there
are other miscellaneous writings and fragments
from various sources, some of which are of very
doubtful authenticity. The Doctrine of the Contemplative Life, the Incorruptibility of the World,
and two very interesting works, that Against Flac-
cus, giving an account of the persecutions to which
the Jews were subject, and that on The Virtues
and on the office of Ambassadors, addressed to
Caius, giving an account of the embassy to Rome,
of which Philo formed part.

It will not be possible, in our brief space, to describe all these writings. There is a great deal of repetition and verbiage in them, which, to our modern ideas, render them tedious and almost unreadable, but they are of great value as indicating the method and spirit of the School of which Philo was the greatest representative. The first thing that strikes us in these works is the intimacy displayed in them with Greek philosophy and literature. They are full of allusions to the poets of Greece, and the phraseology employed is frequently that of the philosophical systems. The names of sixty-four different Greek writers occur in Philo's pages. It is evident that he had studied the works of Plato and Aristotle, and that he knew familiarly the later systems of Greek philosophy. But at the same time, Philo does not write as an advocate of any of these systems. His object is not to adduce Scripture for their support. The underlying principle in all his comments on the Old Testament is that of a universal truth communicated to men in every age and every nation, in greater or less degree, but pre-eminently revealed in the books of Moses. It is very evident that he reads into the words of the Pentateuch the ideas which he has derived from the speculations of heathen philosophers, with the intention of show-

ing that whatever truth has been discovered was
given by God to His ancient people, the Jews, and
is laid up in their Scriptures. As an example of
this we may quote the following words from his
commentary on the first chapter of Genesis.
Having referred to the foundation of great cities
and states, in the imagination of a ruler, he says,
"We must form a somewhat similar opinion of
God, who, having determined to found a mighty
state, first of all conceived its form in his mind,
according to which form he made a world per-
ceptible only by the intellect, and then completed
one visible to the external senses, using the first
one as a model" (chap. iv.) This, of course, is
Platonism applied to the interpretation of Genesis,
and the treatise from which it is taken is full of
the same kind of thought. His use of the term
νοῦς—intellect, as the central part of the soul, as he
calls it, the soul of the soul, is thoroughly Platonic.
"Let no one think that he is able to judge of the
likeness of man to God from the characters of the
body; for neither is God a being with the form of
a man, nor is the human body like the form of
God; but the resemblance is spoken of with reference to the most important part of the soul,
namely, the mind (νοῦς); for the mind which exists
in each individual has been created after the like-

ness of that one Mind which is in the universe as
its primitive model, being in some sort the God of
that body which carries it about and bears its image
within it" (chap. xxiii.) Like all the philosophic
writers of that time, Philo laboured hard to be rid
of what he and others dreaded so much—anthropomorphism. It seemed to him that all human speech
with respect to the Divine nature hides it from the
intellect, and that it is the work of the philosopher
to penetrate through the veil of language, and discover that which is beyond it, the absolute truth
of the Divine. It must be remembered that Philo
had the Greek Bible in his hands, and in that there
is a very evident tendency to soften down the old
Hebraic methods of speech into harmony with Greek
modes of thought. It was this philosophical spirit
which lay at the foundation of the allegorical treatment of the Old Testament, which, while it can
be traced much earlier than Philo, was certainly
wrought out most fully by him. There must be a
meaning beyond and behind the letter of Scripture.
"The letter of the text must be held fast; and
biblical personages and historians were real. But
only narrow-minded slaves of the letter would stop
here; the more so, as sometimes the literal meaning alone would be tame, even absurd; while the
allegorical interpretation gave the true sense, even

though it might run counter to the letter. Thus, the patriarchs represented states of the soul; and whatever the letter might bear, Joseph represented one given to the fleshly, whom his brothers rightly hated; Simeon, the soul, aiming after the higher; the killing of the Egyptian by Moses, the subjugation of passion, and so on " (Edersheim). It is for the purpose of discipline, and for the sake of those who are of a lower order of mind, that these anthropomorphic representations are employed. And the duty of those who seek after truth is to lay aside that which is only due to the evil of man's heart, and retain that which may be discovered under the literal meaning. If there is anything unworthy of Deity recorded, that must be put aside. Sometimes special and profound meanings are indicated by the modification of words and by minute particles, and changes which seem, at first sight, meaningless. Philo, like many others of the later Jews, believed in the Divine authority of the Septuagint; he therefore lays stress on the Greek meanings of words, and ventures, at times, on changes in the letters, in order to bring out the significance desired. It will be evident that such a method is most dangerous when applied to the Word of God. It became so to the Christian Church, in subsequent ages, and the Alexandrian

School, which may be said to have built itself up to a great extent on the writings of Philo, prepared the way for much of the corrupt teaching of the Middle Ages. The Gnostic errors of the Church may have been derived from Persian sources originally, but the mingling of Eastern theosophy with Christian teaching found very great assistance in the Alexandrian method, which Philo may be said to have given to the second century.

With respect to the particular views which may be found in Philo's writings, it is only right to acknowledge that, side by side with that which is false and injurious, there are occasionally passages of great beauty and great elevation of moral feeling, showing that the general sentiment which possessed the mind of this philosophical Jew was one of reverence for the Word of God and for the comparatively pure standard which is put before us in the Law of Moses. He seems to be a kind of Eclectic in his doctrine of the Divine nature—God is to be distinguished from the material world; He is without qualities and unchangeable; He is infinitely above man, and therefore cannot be defined in any terms of human life or expression. But then, again, he seems to believe in a doctrine of Immanence, following the teaching of the Stoics. He is *One and All.* The world is the realm of

o

God. When he comes to explain how this Divine Person has wrought out the world, he very plainly teaches the Gnostic doctrine of demons or lower powers and rulers of the material world. Speaking of the words used in Genesis i. 26, "Let us make man," he says they show that God "assumed other beings to Himself as assistants, in order that, as the Governor of all things, He might have all the blameless intentions and actions of man, when he does right, attributed to Him ; and that His other assistants might bear the imputation of his contrary actions ; for it was fitting that the Father should, in the eyes of His children, be free from all imputation of evil and vice and energy in accordance with sin and evil" (xxiv.)

There are two points, however, which must be touched upon in this notice of Philo before we pass away from him. He may have derived some of his notions from Rabbinical sources. His doctrine of the Logos certainly has more affinity to the teaching of the Rabbis than to that of the Apostle John, who is supposed by some to have borrowed from him. Both these points have been dwelt upon at some length by Dr. Edersheim. "There is an analogy," he says, "between his teaching and that of Jewish Mysticism, as ultimately fully developed in the 'Kabbalah.' The very term

Kabbalah (from *Kabal,* to hand down) seems to point out not only its *descent* by oral tradition, but also its *ascent* to ancient sources. Its existence is presupposed and its leading ideas are sketched in the Mishnah. The Targums also bear at least one remarkable trace of it. May it not be that as Philo frequently refers to ancient traditions, so both Eastern and Western Judaism may here have drawn from one and the same source—we will not venture to suggest how high up—while each made use of it as suited their distinctive wants ? Neither Eastern mystical Judaism nor the philosophy of Philo could admit of any direct contact between God and creation. The Kabbalah solved the difficulty by their *Sephiroth* or emanations from God, through which the contact was ultimately brought about, and of which the *En-soph,* or crown, was the spring, the source from which the infinite light issued. If Philo found greater difficulties, he had also more ready help from the philosophical system to hand. His *Sephiroth* were 'Potencies' (δυνάμεις), 'words' (λόγοι), intermediate powers ;—'Potencies,' we imagine, when viewed Godward ; 'words,' as used creationwards. They were not emanations, but, according to Plato, 'archetypal ideas,' on the model of which all that exists was formed ; and also, according to the Stoic idea, the cause of all, pervading all, forming all, and sustaining all. Then these Potencies were wholly in God, and yet wholly out of God. If we divest all this of its philosophical colouring, did not Eastern Judaism also teach that there was a distinction between the Unapproachable God and God Manifest?" A connection between the two doctrines may also be traced in the view given of the moral character of God. He is Elohim, the God of justice, and Jehovah, the God of mercy, according to the Jewish teachers. "Philo places, next to the Divine Word, *goodness* as the creative potency, and *power* as the ruling potency. He saw these two potencies in the two cherubims, and in the two angels which accompanied the Divine Word when on His way to destroy the cities of the plain." He enumerates other potencies, but the great point is that he regards them as intermediate between the Divine Essence and the world, media through which revelation was made.

Philo's doctrine of the Logos is a mixture of philosophical and scriptural ideas. "In Talmudical writings we find mention not only of the *Shem* or 'Name,' but also of the 'Shechinah,' God as manifest and present, which is sometimes also presented as the Holy Spirit. But in the Targums we meet with yet another expression, which, strange to say, never occurs in the Talmud. It is that of the *Memra,* Logos, or 'Word.' Not that the term is exclusively applied to the Divine Logos. But it stands out as perhaps the most remarkable fact in this literature that God—not as in His permanent manifestation or manifest Presence, but as revealing Himself—is designated *Memra.* Altogether, that term, as applied to God, occurs in the Targum Onkelos 179 times, in the so-called Jerusalem Targum 99 times, and in the Targum Pseudo-Jonathan 321 times. A critical analysis shows that in 82 instances in Onkelos, in 71 instances in the Jerusalem Targum, and in 213 instances in the Targum Pseudo - Jonathan, the designation *Memra* is not only distinguished from God, but evidently refers to God as revealing Himself. But what does this imply? The distinction between God and the *Memra of Jehovah* appears in many passages. Equally the *Memra of Jehovah* is distinguished from the *Shechinah.* Nor is it used instead of the word *Jehovah,* nor for the well-known Old Testament expression 'the angel of the Lord,' nor yet for the *Metatron* of the Targum Pseudo-Jonathan and of the Talmud. Does it then represent an old tradition underlying all these? Beyond this, Rabbinical theology has not preserved to us any

doctrine of personal distinction in the Godhead.
And yet, if words have any meaning, the *Memra*
is a hypostasis, though the distinction of permanent,
personal subsistence is not marked. Nor yet, to
complete this subject, is the *Memra* identified
with the Messiah. In the Targum Onkelos distinct mention is twice made of this, while in the
other Targums no fewer than seventy-one biblical
passages are rendered with explicit reference to
Him " (Edersheim, vol. i. pp. 47, 48). The Logos
of Philo, while it may be founded upon these
ancient Jewish ideas, is yet a less definite and more
philosophical conception. It seems to be a com-
bination of the Memra of Onkelos with the Idea
of Plato. It is the archetypal Man, the image of
God, upon which man was made. Philo, no doubt,
endeavoured to find the *"idea"* of the Platonic
philosophy in Scripture, and the Greek Logos was
ready to his hand. The Logos separates the world
from God, and yet unites them as intermediate.
There is, in Philo's language, some degree of resemblance to that of St. John, but it is only
partial. The Logos is interpreter and prophet,
mediator, high priest, taking away the sins of man,
and by His intercession procuring for us the mercy
of God. He is even called the Paraclete, the Sun,
the Manna of the soul, the Indwelling Word, the

Melchizedek, King of Righteousness and King of Peace. But this Logos imparts itself to the true and the good, not to the sinful. He is not a person, but rather reason personified. The mind of the philosopher is evidently struggling with thoughts which are too great for him. He is not yet delivered from the pride of intellect which led so many of the ancient thinkers into error. There is no compassion for the ignorant and for them that are out of the way in such a doctrine; it is a doctrine for the elect souls, *i.e.*, for the wise men apart from the multitude. But such gropings after truth, so close upon the time of our Saviour's Advent, are exceedingly instructive. The horizon of the Jewish Church was brighter in the West than in the East. Such men as Philo were witnesses for God. They testified at once to the vast superiority of the Mosaic revelation to the confused thinkings of the heathen, and to the hope which was treasured up in the Jewish Scriptures, destined to appear in a new light, again rising in the Eastern sky—the dawn of an eternal day.

CHAPTER XI.

THE DAWNING LIGHT.

WE have already described the growth of the Messianic expectation and the very extraordinary development of it in the last century before Christ.   Our review of the history has brought us very near to the time when the promised revelation should be made—when the great Deliverer should come, who should fulfil the desire of the Jewish people and confirm the covenant made to the fathers.   It has been remarked in a former place that there were great differences among those who entertained the same expectation of a personal advent.   "Some were mere political zealots and dreamers, others were deeply religious students of the Word of God, and Israelites indeed, like Nathanael."   It is of the utmost importance to keep in mind this distinction as we approach the time of our Lord.   The question naturally suggests itself to the outsider, why was Jesus Christ rejected, if the people were full of the anticipation that their Messiah would appear? The answer is a very simple and sufficient one. Under the influence of Rabbinical teaching, the bulk of the nation was blinded to the true conception of the promised deliverance. They allowed the political circumstances of the times, which were depressing to their national pride, to obscure, not to say obliterate, the true spiritual elements of the Old Testament prediction. No doubt even the Rabbis expected a great Teacher and religious Reformer. But they indulged in most exaggerated language with respect to the Messiah's triumph over His enemies and the splendour of His kingdom, without recognising the true connection of such hopes with the principles of Divine revelation. They were very partial and prejudiced in their study of the Old Testament. The cross of Christ was a stumbling-block to them, simply because they would not see it in the prophetic writings which they acknowledged — because they could not, in their spiritual blindness, reconcile it with the prospect which they dwelt upon of victory and worldly glory.

But it would be a great mistake to suppose that there were no exceptions to this wide-spread perversion of the Jewish mind. The synagogues were under the influence of the Rabbis. The

Rabbis no doubt were chiefly guided by the traditional views which were enforced upon them by
their leaders.   The tone of the Sanhedrim at Jerusalem would be given to all the synagogues, more
or less, throughout the land.   But times of great
national suffering and depression generally favour
independence of thought and individuality of character.   The religious life of the people is called
out into more practical expression.   "They that
fear the Lord speak often one to another."   The
humbler worshippers in the sanctuary have their
minds awakened to attend to the signs of the
times.   The Scriptures are the ready resort of such
inquirers.   They have no opportunity of mingling
with the great and learned.   In their own homes
and in the privacy of their own chambers they
are asking the question, "O Lord, how long!
When shall the salvation of Israel come out of
Zion?"   It will be well to give a closer attention
to those few, but by no means insignificant, indications which we find in the opening pages of the
Gospel narrative of the existence among the people
of Palestine, immediately previous to the birth of
our Lord, of a devout and simple-minded study of
the ancient predictions and an expectation founded
upon it, not of mere political change and external
splendour, but of that which in the best sense

would be "*the consolation*" of the true Israel,
their rising to their Divine vocation, and becoming
the Light of the world.

Our first glance at the religious condition of
Palestine must be directed to the capital, the
centre of the national life. There we find, in the
midst of a seething mass of political and ecclesiastical strife, a small group of watching and waiting souls, upon whom the first rays of the new
day fell with wonderful quickening power, as upon
a true germ of a new birth, a "remnant according
to the election of grace," the initial Kingdom of
Heaven, which was soon to be proclaimed as "at
hand." There was, as has been pointed out by
Dr. Edersheim and others, a strange mixture of
two worlds in Jerusalem. It was not only a Greek
and Hebrew world which there came together, the
influence of Gentile thought and Jewish traditionalism, but "piety and fidelity also." "The
devotion of the people and the liberality of the
rich were unbounded. Fortunes were lavished on
the support of Jewish learning, the promotion of
piety, or the advance of the national cause. Thousands of their offerings and the costly gifts in the
Temple bore evidence of this. If priestly avarice
had artificially raised the price of sacrificial animals,
a rich man could bring into the Temple at his own

cost the number requisite for the poor. Charity was not only open-handed, but most delicate, and one who had been in good circumstances would be actually enabled to live according to his former condition." Painful evidence comes to us of the luxuriousness at Jerusalem at that time, and of the moral corruption to which it led. But, notwithstanding that ritualism was at its height and morality in a very low state among the people, there is very interesting evidence in the sacred narrative of a real and vigorous spiritual life among select souls. Scarcely sufficient attention has been paid by students of Scripture to the remarkable fact that there was a prophetess residing in some precinct of the Temple, who was not only revered because of her great age and Nazarite-like devotion, but who would seem to have been specially inspired and gifted with prophetic insight and speech. *" There was one* ANNA, *a prophetess, the daughter of Phanuel, of the tribe of Aser: she was of a great age, and had lived with an husband seven years from her virginity. And she was a widow of about fourscore years and four, which departed not from the Temple, but served God with fastings and prayers night and day."* She must have been at least a hundred and six years old. It is certain, therefore, that she would be well acquainted with the popular expectations with respect to the coming of the Messiah. She probably devoted herself to a life of prayer and religious vigils with the feeling of special preparation for the coming manifestation. Her life was one of singular and most lofty self-consecration. It is not likely that one so distinguished would have remained altogether silent for so many years. Her designation of prophetess points to her having been visited by the Spirit, and having spoken to the people, perhaps, on many occasions. This is rendered the more probable from the fact that when she recognised, under inspiration, the birth of the Messiah, she immediately resumed her prophetic office, though at so advanced an age, and not only lifted up her voice in a prophetic strain of praise and thanksgiving, but *"spoke of Him to all those that looked for redemption in Jerusalem."* How large was her audience we cannot say, but it must have been more than those who were gathered in the Temple at the time of the Saviour's presentation. The fact that she could speak to *"all those who looked for redemption,"* that her voice would be heard by many, is full of significance. There was a band of faithful souls in the midst of that corrupt population. Another reading, which has been followed in the Revised Version, leaves it an open question whether the address of Anna was delivered to more than those in the Temple. "She spoke of Him to all them that were looking for the redemption of Jerusalem." But yet another reading would substitute "*Israel*" for "*Jerusalem*." So that any way the reference may be taken as capable of a wide interpretation. Such a prophetess would not be likely to limit her address to a single occasion. The very name *Anna* is suggestive. The mother of Samuel was herself an inspired woman, and heralded with her prophetic word the dawn of a very bright period in the religious history of the population. After the long silence of hundreds of years, it was a striking fact that the lips of the aged widow should be opened. The people of Jerusalem must have been startled, and led to think that wonderful times were near.

Side by side with *Anna the Prophetess* stands the venerable *Simeon*. He is introduced, not as a prophet, but as one of the " *devout*," who at any time might be inspired to communicate a Divine message. There are other instances in Scripture in which prophetic words have come forth suddenly from those who were not trained and recognised as prophets. " *Behold, there was a man in Jerusalem whose name was Simeon, and the same man was just and devout, waiting for the consolation of*

Israel, and the Holy Ghost was upon him. And it was revealed to him by the Holy Ghost that he should not see death before he had seen the Lord's Christ; and he came by the Spirit into the Temple, and when the parents brought in the child Jesus to do for Him after the custom of the Law, then took he Him up in his arms, and blessed God, and said, Lord, now lettest Thou Thy servant depart in peace, according to Thy word, for mine eyes have seen Thy salvation, which Thou hast prepared before the face of all people; a light to lighten the Gentiles, and the glory of Thy people Israel" (Luke ii. 25–32). Here there are several points which are remarkable. Simeon not only waited for consolation, but he waited for a person in whom that consolation would be ministered. He was not only under the influence of a pervading expectation, but he had a special revelation sent to him by which the prospect was brought within the scope of his own life. Under the direct, supernatural guidance of the Spirit he went into the Temple, and the familiar sight of parents presenting their child before the Lord was immediately lifted up in his mind into the sphere of fulfilled prophecy, so that he could see the Divine Deliverer in a sleeping infant. Then another important feature of that interesting crisis was the spiritual, elevated utterances of this Old Testament saint, standing, as it were, on the meeting-point of the two economies, departing in peace with the sight of the rising Sun, but under the inspiration of the moment foretelling the character of the coming day. The salvation which is now already on the horizon is " *before the face of all people* " (κατὰ πρόσωπον πάντων τῶν λαῶν). It is " *a light to lighten the Gentiles* " (φῶς εἰς ἀποκάλυψιν ἐθνῶν), " *and the glory of Thy people Israel.*" And to Mary, Simeon spake, wrapping up an inspired prediction in his fatherly blessing on the parents and their Child. " *Behold this child is set* (κεῖται) *for the fall and rising again of many in Israel ; and for a sign which shall be spoken against (yea, a sword shall pierce through thy own soul also), that the thoughts of many hearts may be revealed.*" It would be difficult to find a shorter summary of the leading characteristics of Messiah's kingdom than in this swanlike song of the dying Simeon. The universality of the Gospel is there. The cross is there. The Divine judgments coming into Israel with the Great Day of the Lord which had now dawned. The brightness of the new kingdom casting out all the darkness of human error and the clouds of ignorance and doubt. The glorious new Israel coming forth in this Child, whose personality shall be the starting-point of the regenerated race. They

were all, if not distinctly visible, yet dimly revealed to the prophetic vision of this saint. His
voice was an anticipation of the voice from heaven
which subsequently testified to the Beloved Son in
whom the Father was well pleased. Now if such a
man as Simeon was to be found in Jerusalem at the
time of our Saviour's birth, and for years before, we
cannot doubt that there was much of prayerful,
devout, and even inspired thought and utterance
among the religious people of the capital. No
doubt the revelations of the Spirit came to those
who were highest in their religious life, least under
the influence of the deadening ritualism and traditionalism of the time; but the account which the
Evangelist gives us of Simeon and Anna does not
exclude the supposition that they were surrounded
by a number of kindred spirits, who were waiting
with them for the first streaks of light on the
horizon, that they might hail them with thanksgiving and praise. To such an ecclesia, in the
midst of the moral wilderness of Jerusalem, messages of grace were sent from time to time, and
faith was thus maintained.

But we must now look away from the central
point of Judaism, and attend to other instances of
the same Divine work of preparation among the
Jewish people—instances which prove to us that it

P

was work spread over the whole land from north to
south. The hill country of Judea was separated
from Jerusalem by no great distance, but it was
distinguished from it by the broad difference of
peasant life from that of a metropolis, and the
simplicity of a secluded pastoral country from a
city peculiarly exposed to excitements, both political
and ecclesiastical. Zacharias and Elizabeth were
very different from such priests and their wives, as
would often be seen in Jerusalem. The Rabbis and
the learned priests of the great city would look
down on such a man. He would be regarded as a
rustic priest, and by some treated even with contempt. But what kind of piety was at that time
not uncommon in these rural districts, we can see
from the study of that devout couple, *"both righteous before God, and walking blameless in all the
commandments and ordinances of the Lord."* The
shepherds of the neighbourhood of Bethlehem *"keeping watch over their flocks by night,"* to whom the
angelic appearance came, and upon whom the glory
of the Lord descended, shining round about them,
must have been pious watchers for the signs of the
coming Redeemer, or they would not have received
the heavenly announcement, neither would they
have gone at once to see the great sight in Bethlehem. They became the first preachers of the glad

tidings, and were doubtless filled with the influence of the Holy Ghost, that they might fulfil aright such a mission. It must not be forgotten when we are thinking of these rural districts of Palestine, that the synagogue worship, which, since the time of Ezra, had spread through the land, was a great help to the religious life of the people ; and we can easily understand that when the Temple, with its magnificent ritual, was out of reach, the study of the Scriptures and the simple explanations of the synagogue could feed the minds of those whose hearts were open to Divine grace. So that there would be many scattered through the country who were like Zacharias and Elizabeth, and Joseph and Mary, and the shepherds—ready to follow the leading of the Spirit. It is said that in Jerusalem itself there were as many as four hundred and eighty synagogues, and there would be one in every community where there were ten families gathered together. Speaking of the general diffusion of religious influences in Palestine, Dean Stanley says, "Nothing is more difficult than to detect the popular sentiment of a nation apart from its higher culture and its public events. Yet in this case it is not impossible. For the first time we are now entering on a period when 'the people of the land,' the peasants of Palestine, found a

voice in the literature and took a part in the
struggles of the nation. In the provincial towns
the system of schools had kept alive the knowledge
of the sacred books, though often of another class
than those studied in the capital. The parables
and riddles with which, even in the grave colleges,
the teachers were wont to startle their drowsy
hearers into attention, were yet more congenial
amongst the rural villagers. Instead of the tedious
controversies of legal ministry which agitated the
theologians at Jerusalem, the Prophets, with their
bright predictions, were studied or read in the
synagogues. Instead of the *Halacha*, or the
authoritative rule for legal action, the rustic or
provincial teachers threw themselves on the *Haggadha*, the 'legendary' or the poetical branch of
the Scriptures. The Talmudical writers never
mention the Haggadists—the Haggadists rarely
mention the Talmudists; but not the less truly
did they exist side by side." The inspiration which
was poured out on such simple-minded people
would correspond with their accustomed thoughts.
They were familiar with the Psalms and the Prophets, and the utterances which came forth from
their lips were steeped in the very spirit of the Old
Testament psalmody and prophecy. Dr. Edersheim has shown that the hymn of Zacharias closely

corresponds with ancient Jewish prayers, but those prayers were derived from the prophets. "This analogy between the hymn of Zacharias and the prayers of Israel will best appear from the benediction with which these eulogies closed. For, when thus examined, their leading thoughts will be found to be as follows :—God as the *shield of Abraham*; He that raises the dead, and causes *salvation to shoot forth*; the Holy One; who graciously giveth knowledge; who taketh pleasure in *repentance*; who multiplieth forgiveness; who *redeemeth Israel*; who healeth their (spiritual) diseases; *who blesseth the years*; who *gathereth the outcasts of His people*; *who loveth righteousness and judgment*; who is *the abode and stay of the righteous*; *who buildeth Jerusalem*; who causeth *the Horn of Salvation* to shoot forth; who *heareth prayer*; who *bringeth back the Shechinah to Zion*; *God the gracious One*, to whom praise is due; who *blesseth His people Israel with peace*" (vol. i. p. 159). The pious priest was familiar with such language, and it only needed that his mind should be lifted up by Divine communications and by the miraculous events which had occurred, that he should pour forth his hymn of praise full of the feeling of a great time, when that which was "*spoken by the mouth of the holy prophets*" should come to pass, the *"promised mercy"* should be performed, *"the holy covenant"* remembered, *"the oath"* divinely kept. The vision was before the mind of the inspired man, the herald preparing the way of the Lord, *"the dayspring from on high giving light to them that sit in darkness and in the shadow of death, and guiding the feet of the true Israel into the way of peace."*

We have referred to the religious life of the hill country of Judea, twenty miles from Jerusalem. Galilee, in the north, was more remote from the central point of Jewish life, and its people were different in physical and mental characteristics from the people of the south ; but when we think of Nazareth we can have no hesitation in believing that in Galilee also there were elect souls, chosen vessels, into which the gracious influences of the Divine Spirit were poured, not by means outside the channels of the Old Testament, but through them by their sanctified use. It would be a great mistake to represent Nazareth as entirely cut off from intercourse with Jerusalem, as a mere secluded country town where rustic ignorance shut up its inhabitants within a narrow circle of ideas, and the constraints of poverty and toil "froze the genial currents of their souls." It was not so—Nazareth was on the highway of commerce, and it was the meeting-place of priests on their road to the Temple. "Men of all nations busy with another life than that of Israel, would appear in the streets of Nazareth ; and through them thoughts, associations, and hopes connected with the great outside world would be stirred. But, on the other hand, Nazareth was also one of the great cities of Jewish Temple life. The priesthood was divided into twenty-four courses, which in turn ministered in the Temple. The priests of the course which was to be on duty always gathered in certain towns, whence they went up in company to Jerusalem, while those of their number who were unable to go spent the week in fasting and prayer. Now Nazareth was one of those priest - centres, and although it may well have been that comparatively few in distant Galilee conformed to the priestly regulations, some must have assembled there in preparation for the sacred functions, or appeared in its synagogue. Even the fact, so well known to all, of the living connection between Nazareth and the Temple, must have wakened peculiar feelings" (Edersheim).

In addition to these associations with the world and with the Temple, which would be felt more or less by all the inhabitants of the little town, the Davidic descent, the consciousness of a fleshly bond with the favoured family, acted powerfully no doubt upon the feelings of that group of pious people, who there waited for the consolation of Israel. Both Joseph and Mary were directly descended from David, and nearly related to one another. No historical details have come down to us with respect to the early life of the Virgin. But we cannot require them. When she first appears in the sacred narrative, she appears as one full of theocratic feeling, highly favoured, in a state of deep spiritual recipiency. "The handmaid of the Lord." She is not only pious in the sense of obedience to the Divine commands, and observant of religious ordinances, but she is in a very elevated state of mind, thinking much of the Messiah and His kingdom, possibly thinking of herself as one who, being in the line of David, might be chosen of the Lord to be His anointed priestess.

It has been observed by Dr. Lange that "such hearts as were to be capable of welcoming and receiving the highest revelation of grace in its bodily manifestation, had to be prepared not merely by the bestowal of noble dispositions, but by their development—not merely in the School of Israelite doctrine, but of Israelite experience. They had to be thoroughly unhappy in the truest sense, to be brought to despair of the goodness of

the old exterior world, and to experience, in the
annihilation of their former ideals, the judgment of
God upon its sinfulness, in which they also saw its
misery and sadness. Thus only could they have
given up those false notions of a Messiah which
were the ruin of their nation; thus alone have
known the happiness of receiving, with a poverty
of spirit deep in their knowledge of the world, the
Prince of the Heavenly Kingdom, who was to
change judgment into salvation, and to build up
a new world on the ruins of the old." We must
suppose Mary to have passed through such an
experience. There may have been something in
her personal circumstances, in her connection with
Joseph, that quickened the work of Divine grace
in maturing her soul for the higher revelations
which were to be vouchsafed her. It may be, as
Dr. Lange has suggested, that Joseph did not
understand her in her deepest experiences—" She
was unceasingly feeling the sad condition of the
House of David and of Israel, which was so secretly
forming into a judgment upon the inner life of the
solitary heart. But, like a true daughter of Israel,
she anointed her face; from the burnt sacrifice in
which she offered up her first dreams of life and of
the world, to the great Israelite duty of legal obedience, she came forth as the virgin, in whom the

new world was to have its beginning, the promise
of the Redeemer to work with the Divine creative
power, in whose womb the Gospel was to assume
flesh and blood." It is exceedingly interesting, in
illustration of this view—that Mary was especially
prepared by the Spirit of God for the revelations
to be made to her—to study her *Magnificat* in the
light of the Old Testament. She made haste,
when the annunciation of the angel Gabriel was
made to her, to visit her kinswoman, in the hill
country of Judea. The two women stood in each
other's presence as mutual witnesses to the truth
of the Divine Word, beaming in each other's eyes
with the light of the celestial world. It has been
well said of the sacred music which burst forth in
that house of Zacharias, " It was the antiphonal
morning - psalmody of the Messianic Day as it
broke, of which the words were still all of the Old
Dispensation, but their music of the New; the
keynote being that of ' favour,' ' grace,' struck by
the Angel in his first salutation; ' favour ' to the
virgin; ' favour,' eternal ' favour' to all His humble
and poor ones; and ' favour ' to Israel, stretching
in golden line from the calling of Abraham to the
glorious future that now opened. Not one of these
fundamental ideas but lay chiefly within the range
of the Old Testament; and yet all of them now lay

beyond it, rather in the golden light of the new day" (Edersheim). Referring to the *Magnificat*, it has been often remarked that it was founded upon Hannah's song of praise and thanksgiving, which we find in 1 Sam. ii. 1–10. Possibly, therefore, it had been the growth of many days of meditation and prayer and study of the Scriptures under the influence of the Spirit of God. It may have been an immediate inspiration, or composed during the three months of Mary's residence with Elizabeth. However we regard it, it is certain that it is derived from the Old Testament, and breathes the very spirit of Old Testament piety. No one can doubt that the Psalms and the prophets, together with the Pentateuch, were all familiar to Mary's mind. Even the personal reference is borrowed. "*From henceforth all generations shall call me blessed.*" This was little more than an application to herself of the ancient words of Leah (Gen. xxx. 13). "And Leah said, Happy (blessed) am I, for the daughters will call me blessed" (cf. Prov. xxxi. 28; Matt. iii. 12; James v. 11), together with a remembrance of the angel's words, "*Blessed art thou among women,*" "*Hail, highly favoured!*" And yet, at the same time, Mary's *Magnificat* is truly from herself, it is thoroughly original. The circumstances in Hannah's case and her own were

somewhat similar. It was "the lot of the poor,
the despised, the oppressed," as it has been well
said by Lange, "that she experienced, and especially of those rejected ones who bear in their hearts
the nobility of a higher vocation, of deeper reflection, and greater devotedness of life. She went,
during her journey from Nazareth to Judea, to visit
Elizabeth, who looked upon herself as a princess of
such rejected ones. The greeting of her friend and
relative gave to her a higher assurance. She now
sees the whole world glitter in the sunshine of that
grace which raises the rejected ; that realm of glory
to which God elects the humble and lowly was now
displayed before her eyes. She had a presentiment
of the Good Friday and Easter Day of her Son."

Truly this was the dawning Light. The Kingdom was already sketched in outline by the hand
of this lowly woman. "*The strength which scat-
tereth the proud, putteth down the mighty from
their seats, is the strength which is mercy to them
that fear Him from generation to generation ;
exalting those of low degree, filling the hungry with
good things, helping His servant Israel in remembrance of His mercy, as He spake unto our fathers,
to Abraham and to his seed for ever.*" Much as
we deprecate the superstitious use which has been
made of the name of the Virgin, it is impossible to

contemplate such a piety as hers, coming forth out
of the Old Testament, and not acknowledge that so
fair a flower was worthy of the soil in which it
grew. No human art can ever do justice to it.
By looking closely at that lovely blossom out of
the Dispensation which was passing away, we are
prepared to hail the advent of Him who gathered
up all the past into Himself, who at once satisfied
the yearning which the ages of revelation had left
behind them in the heart of man, and opened a
new Kingdom, a Kingdom of Heaven to all believers. The light first came upon the horizon in
the varied colours and broken lines of personal and
individual character, scattered all along the land of
Palestine from Jerusalem and the hill country to
the south of it, to Galilee and the romantic neighbourhood of its beautiful sea, but when thirty years
had gone by the morning twilight had grown into
the manifest beginning of the Day. We shall complete this review of the interval between the last
of the prophets and the ministry of our Lord by a
short study of that prophetic messenger whose appearance in the wilderness awakened the whole
land of Israel to the rising of the Sun of Righteousness in the heavens.

CHAPTER XII.

THE VOICE IN THE WILDERNESS.

THE state of the Jewish Church at the time of our Lord's birth was not that of complete indifference to the horizon which was before it. We have seen that there were watchers on the heights of faith, who looked forth prayerfully and with eager gaze for the first indications of the " dawning Light." There was a scattered seed through the land, which promised a renewed spiritual life, when the time to pour out the blessing came and the believers should be multiplied. Although the small band of humble people connected with Nazareth and the hill country of Judea, may have drawn to themselves others who, under the influence of the wonderful facts connected with the birth of Jesus and John, were quickened into lively expectation—yet we have no reason to suppose that during the thirty years which intervened between the nativity and the public appearance of our Saviour, there was anything which could be called

a widespread "stirring among the dry bones." The
condition of Palestine, social, political, religious,
grew worse during that generation, instead of
better. The Roman sway under Tiberius was
much more oppressive than under Augustus. "The
first procurator whom Tiberius appointed over
Judea, changed the occupancy of the high priesthood four times, till he found in Caiaphas a sufficiently submissive instrument of Roman tyranny.
The exactions, and the reckless disregard of all
Jewish feelings and interests, might have been
characterised as meeting the extreme limit, if worse
had not followed when Pontius Pilate succeeded to
the procuratorship. Venality, violence, robbery,
persecutions, wanton, malicious insults, judicial
murders, without even the formality of a legal process, and cruelty—such are the charges brought
against his administration. If former governors
had, to some extent, respected the religious examples of the Jews, Pilate set them purposely at
defiance; and this not only once, but again and
again, in Jerusalem, in Galilee, and even in Samaria,
until the Emperor himself interposed" (Edersheim).
There was no hope to be found in any of the
established institutions of the land. The schools
of the Rabbis wrangled over mere questions of
ritual or legality. The Scriptures were not ex-

pounded by the Scribes in any new sense to lift up
the hearts of the people with the thought of coming redemption. The political zealots, while they
talked of conspiracies and fanned the flame of
earthly ambition, wrought no change in the dark
cloud of oppression and despondency which hung
over all the land. But there was one name which
still had a magic spell to rouse all classes of the
nation—it was the name "*Messiah*." No one
could hear that name pronounced and not at once
direct a look to the horizon. It will be some day
a great Light shining in the heavens. When He
shall appear all the night of our misery will roll
away like a cast-off vesture, and we shall be clothed
in His brightness as with garments of salvation and
victory. But when and where shall Messiah
appear? It was a question which no doubt was
often agitated among learned Priests and Rabbis,
but which never took any one of them away from
the precincts of the Temple or the synagogue, or
led them to look forth in any new direction for
the sign of His advent. The visitor to the Alpine
summit waits in the dim twilight of early morning to see the glories of the sunrise. He turns his
face towards the east, but he knows not the exact
spot where the first golden streak will appear. At
last the sound of the Alpine horn proclaims the

approach of the great monarch of day. The watcher hails the sight with fixed gaze and glowing admiration. So it was that when the public ministry of the Lord Jesus Christ was about to commence, the herald-prophet was sent to wake up the multitude throughout the whole land, to direct their attention to the right place, and eagerly expect the coming of the Kingdom of Heaven.

But why was the mission of John the Baptist, as a preparatory mission to that of our Saviour, characterised by the novel features which distinguish it both from anything which, for hundreds of years, had been sent to the Jews, and from the ministry of the Christ Himself which it preceded? In order to answer this question aright, let us review the principal facts, in their connection with the subject which has been before us—the Divine leading of the Jewish Church up to the height of their faith.

The first and most striking fact in the account of John the Baptist and his mission, is the entire separation of it from *the old lines* of Judaism, while, at the same time, it is equally distinct from *the new lines* of Christianity. It is a *"Voice in the wilderness."* John was the son of a priest; but he does not commence his ministry from the Temple. He is not a Rabbi, lifting up his voice in the syna-

Q

gogue. He is not a learned Scribe, poring over
the rolls of Scripture. He is not a Sadducee,
mingling among the banquets of the wealthy and
luxurious, and dropping seeds of rationalistic doubt
into the minds of his hearers. Neither can we say
that he represents any sect whatever among the
religious zealots of the time. He is not the emis-
sary of any party. He is not the mouthpiece of
any religious movement or organisation. He is a
man completely by himself, who for some years
had been passing from wilderness to wilderness, for
the purpose of solitary meditation and study, and
also, perhaps, that he might look with his own
eyes upon some of the remarkable religious de-
votees, who had retired into the neighbourhood of
the Dead Sea and the Jordan, and lived lives of
great simplicity and purity. He was certainly
more at home in such places, and among such
people, than in the scenes of strife and religious
bigotry, and dead, corrupting formalism round the
Temple of Jerusalem. There was no nurture for
such a spirit as his to be found among Scribes and
Pharisees, Herodians and Sadducees. Moreover,
the *voice*, if it is to be a voice which shall summon
all Israel to look for the Messiah as the rising Sun
of Righteousness, must be a voice which calls them
away from the old to the new—from Temple, syna-

gogue, and palace, to the horizon of the spiritual
world. This Elijah must come out of the wilderness. He must be a man like neither priest nor
Rabbi. He must break the bondage of custom and
the sleep of self-complacency, and draw out all
classes and conditions of men into the place where
they shall feel that their consciences are open to
the lightning stroke of heaven, and they shall
tremble before God. He must be able to effect a
twofold change—a turning *from* the old ways—a
turning *to* the open gate of the Kingdom. What
were the main features of John's mission, which
made it a special preparation of the people for
Messiah? Let us distinguish the following four
constituents of this remarkable history, regarded as
preparatory to the work of our Lord. (1.) *The
doctrine* which was contained in it, which sum-
marised the teaching of the Old Testament, and
so formed a link between the Old and the New.
(2.) *The baptismal rite*, which was instituted by it,
and which prepared the way for the baptism of the
kingdom of heaven. (3.) *The proclamation*, which
formed its central fact, pointing to the person and
the ministry close at hand. (4.) The striking *self-
abnegation of the man himself*, by a sudden and
complete eclipse denoting all the more conspicuously
the supremacy and uniqueness of the Messiah.

I. It has not been sufficiently recognised that John the Baptist, while he was pre-eminently, no doubt, the preacher of repentance, was, as a herald of the kingdom of God, a "*voice*," repeating in the wilderness the leading notes of the Old Testament. We have but very scanty notices of his discourses, but we have the facts of his ministry before us, and we are able to form a tolerably adequate conception of its effect upon the minds of those who came into the wilderness to listen to the Voice. Now the whole significance of the Old Dispensation lies along these lines, the *priestly* or sacrificial, the *prophetic* or didactic, the *theocratic* or social. The people were imbued with the three ideas represented in those terms, by their institutions, sacred books, the personalities which were vividly in their remembrance, and the incidents of their national life and history. But what they especially needed in the time of their decay and degeneracy was that such ideas should be before their minds in their naked majesty as divine and heavenly. When they heard them preached by a stern, solitary, spiritual man, like John the Baptist, away from all ceremonies and all sanctified buildings, and all political entanglements and disturbances, their souls realised their greatness, they saw that they were the constituents of a kingdom which might, at any moment, be proclaimed in their midst. *Sacrifice* had been, all through the Jewish history, one of the prominent facts of their national life. But did not their own Scriptures tell them that the mere sacrifice of the altar, the mere offering up of bullocks and goats, was not what God required; but that which sacrifice represented and symbolised—a Divine Lamb, a righteousness which was real, perfect righteousness, put in the place of their iniquities, and bringing them back into a state of reconciliation and fellowship with God? That John did preach that, we may feel quite sure, because he both summoned them to repentance before God, as preparatory to the blessings promised in the New Kingdom, and he connected with that summons to repentance the announcement that the Lamb of God was amongst them, who should take away the sin of the world. The effect which was produced by his preaching was very widespread and very wonderful. The people came to him by their thousands and confessed their sins, and in doing so acknowledged that the mere ritualistic repentance in which they had been trusting was not sufficient. There was a better sacrifice required, there was a higher priesthood for which they must look—there was a divine righteousness which must come to them from heaven. If the

aim of John's preaching had been to revive their
faithfulness to the observance of the temple rites,
to make them more Pharisaical and legal, he would
certainly not have chosen the wilderness for his
sphere of ministry.   But the Ritualistic and
Rabbinical party held aloof from him, because
they felt instinctively that such preaching aimed
a heavy blow. at their formalism, and exposed
their hypocrisy.   "Wisdom was justified of her
children."   Again, it was not only the sacrificial
doctrine of the Old Testament which was thus
cleared of its superstitions, and held forth in the
clear light of day, but another great fact to which
Jewish history bore witness—that God by His
Spirit holds intercourse with men and communi-
cates to them His mind and will.   The prophetic vocation was not limited to those who were
especially distinguished as prophets.   The whole
nation was a kingdom of prophets.   *"To them
were committed the oracles of God."*   They were
set apart by a divine calling, and by special
divine gift, to be the light of the world—"to
give light to them that sit in darkness and in the
shadow of death."   The Rabbis had lost this great
truth in their miserable pedantry.   The very conception of personal inspiration was buried in the
obscurity of the past.   It was transferred from

the individual men to the sacred books, which were being dealt with not as the voice of a living God amongst them, but as a mere dead relic of the past, to be worshipped with superstitious reverence and turned into food for intellectual and spiritual pride. For four hundred years there had been no voice among the people, moving freely through the land, and speaking as a voice of God with authority and power. The nearest approach to it had been the outburst of religious zeal and devotion in the family of the Maccabees, but that had very quickly gone out into political and military fanaticism. There was nothing, as we have seen, which could be placed side by side with the ministry of the Old Testament prophets. But John, the son of Zecharias, is manifestly an inspired man. He speaks as with a voice of God. They cannot resist the energy and the faithfulness with which he appeals to their consciences, and calls them to the bar of judgment in the word of God. But John's own personality was by no means the sole testimony to the Truth. It was part of his message that God was about to pour out of His Spirit as He had done of old. He declared that there was One coming immediately, upon whom the Spirit would descend and rest, as a dove, who should be not only *a* word of God, but *the* word of

God—and, moreover, such would be the graciousness of that time that they themselves might be baptized as freely and fully in (or with) that Spirit of God as he baptized them in (or with) the water. It would be a baptism of fire, as well as a baptism of water; that is, it would not only cleanse them, but it would burn up and consume their sins, and make them new creatures, like gold seven times purified. And yet this was very far from all that the Herald had to announce. What was the message of the Old Testament to their nation? Did it not make them a theocracy? Did they not glory in their privilege as God's peculiar people? Did they not esteem their position as much higher than that of all the nations of the earth, because they had Jehovah as their King? And yet what had come of all that Jewish distinction? They were miserable slaves to the Romans. They were held down in iron bondage. There was no hope in anything they possessed except the promises of God. But He who gave the promises is able to fulfil them. He can raise up children to Abraham out of the very stones on the river bank. "Why should you despair? Is it not because you have no faith in spiritual power? because you are looking to the earth, instead of to heaven? The Kingdom of Heaven is at hand. The promises are now about to be fulfilled. God will lift you up as a nation, if you will believe in Him, and restore to you all that you have lost ; and you shall yet be the heralds of His salvation to the whole world." No doubt that Voice in the Wilderness was not as clear and distinct as the voices of Apostles and Evangelists. Jesus declared that "the least in the Kingdom of Heaven was greater" than John the Baptist, because he could not speak like those who had seen and handled the Word of Life. But we must not misconstrue the comparative silence of the record as to John's teaching. He laboured through some months in public preaching. We cannot suppose that his sermons were mere repetitions of the call to repentance. They were intended to prepare the way of the Lord. They were to form a link of connection between the revelations of the Old Testament and the revelations of the New. The chief points of doctrine which were henceforth to be the main lines of the Christian faith, would undoubtedly be the chief tones of the Voice in the Wilderness, thus preparing the people for One who was to be their Priest, their Prophet, and their King. No greater prophet, Jesus said, had been born into the world than John the Baptist, and with such a testimony to his greatness we cannot doubt that he was one who had deeply studied the sacred writings, and who was able under the influence of the Spirit of God to set forth their very substance, in outline at least, before the multitudes. This view of the preaching of John the Baptist will help us to understand what is very often misunderstood, the significance and intention of his baptism, which was not a mere appendage to his preaching, and certainly had no mere personal motive underlying it, but was a distinct preparation for the baptism of the Holy Ghost. To this subject we must now give attention.

II. The baptism of John was an integral part of his mission, and heralded the baptism of the Christian Church. " *Why baptizest thou,*" was the question asked of John by the deputation from the Pharisees, "*if thou be not that Christ, nor Elias, neither that prophet?*" Evidently the Jews connected baptism with some special distinction in the mission of the baptizer. It would seem to them to imply that John regarded himself as in some way a messenger of God, and not a merely ordinary expounder of the Scriptures. The answer which John gave to the question was that the baptism was intended to prepare the way for another person, and, therefore, was only a subordinate baptism; but on other occasions it is described as a baptism "*unto*

the remission of sins" (Mark i. 4; Luke iii. 3).
We are also told that the people were "baptized of
him in Jordan, confessing their sins," Matt. iii. 6.
It did not, therefore, represent by the water the
actual forgiveness and reconciliation with God of
the person baptized, but rather that acknowledgment of sin which accompanied, under the Mosaic
Dispensation, the offering up of sacrifice. It was
entirely an initiatory rite. The baptized person
was regarded as prepared by it for the reception of
the Kingdom of God. We are able, by this view of
the rite, to connect it with the baptisms which were
customary among the Jews. They were ablutions
which preceded or accompanied the act of worship,
but they were not regarded as containing in themselves any gift of God conveyed through the water.
So in the case of John's baptism there is no intention to teach that by baptism the sinner is cleansed
from sin and brought back into a covenant relation
with Jehovah. Such an idea would be inconceiv-
able to the Jewish mind. But those who confessed
their sins and were baptized stood at the altar ready
for the sacrifice. They were prepared to offer it
acceptably. They had already stretched forth their
hands, and it only needed that the Head of the
nation should be revealed unto them that the sacrifice should be complete, and they should rejoice in

the blessings of the Kingdom.   There was a prophetic element, therefore, in the baptism of John,
which gave it its distinctive value.   He said plainly,
There cometh One who taketh away the sin of the
world.   Hence the Baptist was not content to renounce all merit in his baptism, but he, at the same
time, explained it as a mere typical rite which
would be abolished by the fulfilment of its meaning
in the true baptism, the baptism of the Holy Ghost.
The Jews were well able to grasp the meaning of
this, if only they were not blinded by prejudice.
The great day of atonement taught them that sin
was not to be done away by mere words or gifts.
God had promised them to provide a sacrifice.   They
were required to prepare themselves by repentance
and confession for the acceptance of His gift.   We
must avoid the error into which some have fallen,
and amongst them Dr. Stanley, of representing John
as inculcating by his baptism the doctrine of self-
righteousness—that by repentance we enter into the
Kingdom of Heaven.   "He took advantage," says
the Dean, "of that leap into the river or the reser-
voir to call upon one and all to spring into a new
life, to wash off the stains upon their honour and
their consciences, which choked up the pores of
their moral texture and impeded the influx of the
new truths with which the air around them was

shortly to be impregnated. He proclaimed the one indispensable condition of all spiritual religion, that the regeneration of the human spirit was to be accomplished, not by ceremonies or opinions, not by succession or descent, but by moral uprightness. The substitution of the wholesome, inspiriting, simple process of the bath, in which the head and body and limbs should be submerged in the rushing river, for the sanguinary, costly gifts of the sacrificial slaughter-house, was a living representation in a single act of the whole prophetic teaching of the supremacy of Duty!" We quote such words for the sake of pointing out that they are in the very teeth of John's own declarations that he did not baptize with the Holy Ghost, but only prepared the way for One who did. Dr. Stanley refers in a note to the identical use of repentance and regeneration by the early fathers, but he omits to state that IN the Kingdom of God the act of repentance is an act of faith, because the Redeemer has been revealed as an object of faith, but until Christ came repentance was only *unto* the remission of sins which should be declared in the Messiah. The Baptist invited the people to find their salvation in the Lamb of God.

III. The central fact in the Baptist's mission

was his *proclamation of the kingdom.* What, then, was that proclamation? It was the personal testimony of the greatest of all the prophets to the diviner authority of the Lord Jesus Christ. Hence we find it placed in the most prominent position by the fourth Evangelist, who by his profound insight into the truth of the kingdom prepared the way for the conquest of Christianity over the false doctrines which were springing up round the early Church. He begins at once with the fact that the chief errand of the Baptist was " to bear witness of the light, that all men through him might believe." The day after the deputation from the Pharisees had received from the Baptist the solemn renunciation of all claim to be himself the Messiah, and the announcement that already the Great One was in their midst, therefore, while still the multitudes were under the influence of that startling news that Messiah was come, "John seeth Jesus coming unto him, and saith, Behold the Lamb of God, which taketh away the sin of the world. This is He of whom I said, After me cometh a man which is preferred before me : for He was before me. And I knew Him not : but that He should be made manifest to Israel, therefore am I come baptizing with water. And John bare record, saying, I saw the Spirit descending from heaven like a dove, and it abode upon Him. And I knew Him not: but He that sent me to baptize with water, the same said unto me, Upon whom thou shalt see the Spirit descending, and remaining on Him, the same is He which baptizeth with the Holy Ghost. And I saw, and bare record that this is the Son of God." The next day the same proclamation was repeated to disciples, and they were bidden to follow Jesus, which they did, forsaking their master John. The same directness and completeness of the testimony given by John is implied, though not so fully expressed, in the synoptical gospels. The preaching which was the preaching of the Kingdom of God is thus declared to have been a proclamation of the personal Redeemer. In what aspects of His personal character, then, did the Baptist identify, Jesus Christ and the Kingdom of God? He was the Lamb of God. He was the baptizer with the Spirit. He was the Son of God, *i.e.*, the King of Israel. The three essential elements of the Kingdom of God were thus embodied and realised in Christ, the sacrificial atonement which cleansed away sin; the gift of the Divine Spirit which communicated light to those that were in darkness, and life to those that were dead; and the restoration of the fallen state, the rebuilding of Jerusalem, the setting up of

the Throne of Righteousness and Peace in the
world, according to the ancient promise that in
Abraham and his seed all the families of the earth
should be blessed.   It is in this very decided testimony of John to the Messiah that we find the
explanation of the words in which Jesus replied to
the Baptist when he expressed his reluctance to
perform the rite on One so great: "I have need
to be baptized of Thee, and comest thou to me?"
i.e., I have need of the baptism of the Holy Ghost,
and dost Thou who givest the baptism apply for
the baptism which was a preparation for it? Jesus
answered, "Suffer it to be so now, for thus it be-
cometh us to fulfil all righteousness."   You and I
are not acting independently of one another, you
are my witness and I am your Lord.   You give
your witness to me by baptism, and I give my
approval to you by submitting to your baptism.
The Son was baptized not because He was a
penitent but because He was a believer, accepting
before all the people the righteous appointments of
God, and the promises which were contained in
them.   If the baptism of John meant, as Dr.
Stanley maintains, that the person baptized had
passed through repentance into regeneration, it
was a mockery upon the part of the Son of God
to be baptized; but if it meant no more than

acceptance of John's message that the Kingdom of Heaven was at hand, then Jesus was the appropriate subject of such a baptism, and He himself was the most distinguished of John's disciples. But this memorable scene between the Forerunner and the Saviour leads us to the last point to which we have referred.

IV. The Baptist retired into obscurity in view of the manifested Christ. "Rabbi," said the disciples of John, "He that was with thee beyond Jordan, to whom thou barest witness, behold, the same baptizeth, and all men come to Him." It was an important crisis. How did the Baptist meet it? By entire self-abnegation and faithfulness to his own mission. "This my joy is fulfilled." It is the Bridegroom's voice. My voice must be silent, except as the voice of the Bridegroom's friend. "He must increase, but I must decrease." It was in accordance with this retirement of the Baptist that the history records his speedy disappearance by martyrdom from the scene. It would have been a very perplexing state of things had the ministry of John been prolonged, for notwithstanding his distinct announcement of the Messiah, there would have been multitudes who were unable to distinguish between the voice of the Bridegroom and the

R

voice of the Bridegroom's friend. But the work of preparation was now completed. The promised Elijah had come, and for a time the people were willing to rejoice in that light, which was a true light from heaven. But the Day of the Lord is a greater trial of faith than the early morning. The "burning and shining Light" is as nothing when compared to that which the Prophet Malachi said would be "the great and dreadful Day of the Lord," the day which "shall burn as an oven." The horizon of the Jewish Church, on which, as we have seen, there were gleams of light which were never wholly lost for hundreds of years, was henceforth all ablaze with the great facts of the Gospel. Divine righteousness was unveiled. The "going forth" of this Sun of Infinite truth and love "is from the end of the heaven, and His circuit unto the ends of it; and there is nothing hid from the heat thereof."

THE END.

PRINTED BY BALLANTYNE, HANSON AND CO.
EDINBURGH AND LONDON.

NISBET'S THEOLOGICAL LIBRARY.

I.

Crown 8vo.   Price 6s.

IMMORTALITY:

A Series of Papers by the

Rev. Principal CAIRNS, D.D.,

Rev. Canon KNOX-LITTLE, M.A.,

Right Rev. THE BISHOP OF AMYCLA (Coadjutor of H.E. Cardinal MANNING),

Rev. Professor J. RADFORD THOMSON, M.A.,

Rev. EDWARD WHITE,

Rev. J. E. PAGE HOPPS,

Rev. CROSBY BARLOW, M.A.,

And Others.

Reprinted from the Symposium in the Homiletic Magazine.

II.

Crown 8vo.   6s.

ZECHARIAH:

HIS VISIONS AND WARNINGS.

BY THE LATE

REV. W. LINDSAY ALEXANDER, D.D., LL.D., F.R.S.E., EDINBURGH.

III.

Crown 8vo.   6s.

FOUR CENTURIES OF SILENCE;

OR, FROM MALACHI TO CHRIST.

BY THE REV. R. A. REDFORD, M.A., LL.B.,

Professor of Systematic Theology and Apologetics, New College, London ; Author of "The Christian's Plea against Modern Unbelief," &c.

I

IV.

Crown 8vo. 6s.

ATONEMENT:

A Clerical Symposium on the Atonement.

By the Revs. Dr. LITTLEDALE, A. MACKENNAL, J. PAGE HOPPS, Dr. OLVER, Principal RAINY, D.D., EDWARD WHITE, Professor ISRAEL ABRAHAMS, Dr. PATON GLOAG, Ven. Archdeacon FARRAR, Right Rev. BISHOP OF AMYCLA, and Others.

CRITICAL OPINIONS.

The Literary Churchman.

"We recommend our readers to purchase the work. Although the papers are naturally argumentative and not devotional, the record of the effort of different minds to grasp the doctrine of the Atonement cannot but be helpful."

The Irish Ecclesiastical Gazette.

"The volume contains many thoughts of value."

The Literary World.

"A valuable addition to the theological literature of the day."

The Baptist.

"To the trained theologian it will have all the interest of a well-ordered battle between well-trained disputants."

Liverpool Mercury.

"The volume is one of permanent value, and will save both time and research in wading through theological dictionaries to find what lies here ready to hand."

Newcastle Journal.

"We question if any volume has yet been published on the Atonement which sets forth the views of Christendom in so many varied lights, and at the same time with so much mutual toleration and modesty. This is a book which ought to find a place in every theological library."

2

Crown 8vo. 6s.

INSPIRATION:

A Clerical Symposium on In what Sense and Within what Limits is the Bible the Word of God?

By the Ven. Archdeacon FARRAR, the Rev. Principal CAIRNS, the Rev. Prebendary STANLEY LEATHES, D.D., the Rev. Prebendary Row, the Rev. Professor J. RADFORD THOMSON, the Right Rev. the BISHOP OF AMYCLA, and Others.

CRITICAL OPINIONS.

The Church Times.

"The volume is an interesting one, written tnroughout in a temperate and scholarly spirit, and likely to prove useful to the higher stamp of theological students."

The Scotsman.

"These clever papers, written for the most part by men of mark and standing, although they may have an unsettling tendency, are well calculated to attract attention and to repay perusal."

The Freeman.

"Every side of the question is, if not fully, at any rate candidly and reverently discussed; and as an epitome of the various conceptions which are now current on this momentous theme, there can be no better or more useful work than this."

The Literary Churchman.

"If any book were designed to show that the Bible was never intended to stand alone, but that a supernatural revelation must of necessity be committed to a supernatural custodian, it could not have better fulfilled its object than this 'Clerical' Symposium."

The Edinburgh Courant.

"A most valuable contribution to inspirational literature. A great variety of views, all falling within the lines of recognised orthodoxy, are brought together, and made to act and react on each other. Their individual weight is thus more clearly ascertained, and a stronger impression is given of the force of argument in favour of inspiration."

Aberdeen Free Press.

"This valuable and suggestive book ought to have a place in every minister's library."

3

AN EXPOSITORY COMMENTARY ON THE BOOK OF JUDGES.

By the Rev. A. R. FAUSSET, M.A., Editor of Bengel's "Gnomon" in
English, and Author in part of the "Critical and
Experimental Commentary."
Demy 8vo, 10s. 6d.

BY THE SAME AUTHOR.

HORÆ PSALMICÆ. STUDIES IN THE CL. PSALMS:

Their Undesigned Coincidence with the Independent Scripture
Histories Confirming and Illustrating Both.
Second Edition. Demy 8vo, 10s. 6d.

CHRIST AND CHRISTIANITY. ESSAYS.

By PHILIP SCHAFF, D.D., Author of "The Person of Christ," &c.
Demy 8vo, 10s. 6d.

BIBLE HEATHENS.

By the Rev. CHARLES M. GRANT, Dundee.
Crown 8vo, 2s. 6d.

LIGHT IN THE DARKNESS.

By F. WHITFIELD, M.A., Vicar of St. Mary's, Hastings, Author of
"Voices from the Valley," &c.
16mo, 1s. 6d.

SERMONS.

By JOHN GREGG, D.D., late Bishop of Cork.
Second Series. Crown 8vo, 6s.

GATES INTO THE PSALM COUNTRY.

By MARVIN R. VINCENT, D.D.
New Edition. Crown 8vo, 3s. 6d.

THE TEACHING OF THE TWELVE APOSTLES:

A Page of First Century Christian Life, with Translation, Notes,
and Dissertations.
By Canon SPENCE, M.A., Vicar of St. Pancras.
Crown 8vo, 6s.

"Canon Spence's notes are generally excellent. The excursus in this volume are
an able though far from exhaustive treatment of the several points of interest raised
by this treatise."—*Academy.*

THE EMPIRE OF THE HITTITES.

By WM. WRIGHT, D.D.

With Decipherment of Hittite Inscriptions by Professor SAYCE, LL.D.;
A Hittite Map by Col. Sir CHARLES WILSON, F.R.S., and
Captain CONDER, R.E.; and a complete set of Hittite
Inscriptions by W. H. RYLANDS, F.S.A.

Second and Revised Edition, with Additions, and Six New Plates.
Royal 8vo, 17s. 6d.

"Any one who wishes to know more about this remarkable people must read this book, in which Dr. Wright has brought together in a popular form all that has been yet extracted from the various sources that have recently been laid open. Its value is attested by no less an authority than Mr. Gladstone."—*Guardian.*

METAPHORS IN THE GOSPELS:

A Series of Short Studies.

By the Rev. DONALD FRASER, D.D.

Crown 8vo, 6s.

"It will open the eyes of ministers to a fact of which they often seem unaware, that in the Gospels a metaphor is never introduced for the mere purpose of decorating a sentence or gratifying a poetic fancy."—*Daily Chronicle.*

FOR THE WORK OF THE MINISTRY:

A Manual of Homiletical and Pastoral Theology.

By W. G. BLAIKIE, D.D., LL.D., Professor of Apologetics and of Ecclesiastical and Pastoral Theology, New College, Edinburgh.

Fourth Edition. Crown 8vo, 5s.

"A volume which displays a considerable amount of wide and varied reading, much thought and ability, great good feeling, and an earnest and charitable desire to further the attainment of the highest ends of all right human thought and action."—*Guardian.*

BY THE SAME AUTHOR.

THE PUBLIC MINISTRY AND PASTORAL METHODS OF OUR LORD.

Crown 8vo, 6s.

"Should be very acceptable and profitable, not only to those whose life-work is the ministry of the Gospel, but also to those who in other ways take their share of active service for the spiritual good of men, and we heartily commend it to them."—*Messenger.*